JAPANESE SOCIETY

STUDIES IN MODERN SOCIETIES

CONSULTING EDITOR:
CHARLES H. PAGE
University of Massachusetts

A Random House Study in Sociology

JAPANESE SOCIETY

Takeshi Ishida

UNIVERSITY OF TOKYO

RANDOM HOUSE New York

ISBN: 0–394–31011–X

Library of Congress Catalog Card Number: 78–129226

Manufactured in the United States of America. Composed by Westcott & Thomson, Inc.,
Philadelphia, Pa. Printed and bound by Halliday Lithograph Corporation, West Hanover,
Mass.

First Edition
987654321

To Reiko,
Hiroshi, and Ken

Preface

A great many books on Japan have been published in English, but very few of them have been by Japanese authors. This fact in itself is perhaps an indication of the cultural isolation of Japan. Japan exports vast quantities of her material products all over the world but has not, so far, exported many of her cultural products, although not a few Japanese novels have been translated into English and other languages. In Japan's cultural trade there is an excess of imports over exports. This is chiefly due to the fact that in Japan all education is in Japanese, and hence the language barrier that must be surmounted in order to develop mutual exchange of culture with foreign countries is very high.

I am particularly grateful to Random House for giving me an opportunity to improve this situation and to Professor Robert Bellah for recommending me to the publisher and for encouraging and helping me to write this book.

Since the policy of the editor is to ask the authors to write about their own societies, I have tried to produce something different from the books on Japan written by foreign scholars, for, however it is characterized, it is undeniable that there is a difference between the views on Japanese society of Japanese and of Western scholars. There is, of course, a great deal of diversity in Japanese views on Japan, but I have done my best to present views common among Japanese intellectuals.

What is taken for granted among Japanese is not necessarily taken for granted among foreigners. Here again, language poses a problem. Japanese scholars think in terms of Japanese concepts which often cannot be translated satisfactorily into English. It has been very difficult to produce a book with a Japanese point of view that remains readily comprehensible to Western readers.

I would like to express my heartfelt gratitude to Mr. Douglas Anthony and Mr. Graham Healey of Sheffield University for their painstaking correction of my draft. I am also grateful to those friends who spared the time to go through all or part of the draft of this book and make many valuable suggestions: Professor Roger W. Benjamin of the University of Minnesota, Professor Gail Bernstein of the University of Arizona, Professor David Danelski of Yale University, Professor Robert Epp of UCLA, Miss Atsuko Hirai of Harvard University, Mr. Kenneth Sagawa of the University of Wisconsin, Mr. and Mrs. David Sissons of the Australian National University, and Professor Ezra Vogel of Harvard University. I am greatly indebted to Professor Charles H. Page of the University of Massachusetts for his editorial advice and to Mr. Masahiko Iwasaki of the Public Information Bureau, Ministry of Foreign Affairs for his help in providing materials published by the Ministry.

This book could not have been produced without the cooperation of these scholars of different nationalities. I hope that this international cooperation will prove fruitful and that this book will help to promote international understanding.

Tokyo
December 1969   TAKESHI ISHIDA

Contents

Japanese society

SEA OF JAPAN

HOKKAIDO
●Sapporo
●Hakodate

●Sendai
●Niigata

HONSHU
Kanazawa●

Tokyo●
Yokohama● *TOKYO BAY*

●Nagoya
Kyoto●
Kobe● ●Nara ●Shimoda
●Osaka

Hiroshima●

Shimonoseki●

PACIFIC OCEAN

Fukuoka●   SHIKOKU

Nagasaki●

KYUSHU

Kagoshima●

MODERN JAPAN

0 _____ 200 Miles

(Okinawa is not included due to lack of space.)

I

Introduction—Miracle or Misery?

It is often said that Japan has been "successful" in developing herself rapidly. Her economic recovery after defeat in World War II and her recent economic development have been called a "miracle" by many foreign observers.[1] There is no doubt that industrialization has been much faster in Japan than in any other country, not only in the postwar but also in the prewar period (see Figure 1). Japan is now ranked third in the world in terms of Gross National Product, but stands about twentieth in terms of per capita income ($921 in 1967).* It is clear, then, that there are two sides to Japanese society: the miraculously rapid development on the one hand, and the relatively "miserable" circumstances under which the individual lives his daily life on the other. What I want to consider in this book is how these two sides are able to coexist in the same society, and how they have been reconciled.

Japan has much in common with developed Western countries on her "miraculously" developing side, and at the same time much in common with underdeveloped countries on her "miserable" side. As far as possible, I shall try to explain the characteristics of Japanese society by identifying the elements which it has in common with other societies. At the same time, however, it will be necessary to provide

---

* All statistics throughout the book reflect the data available when it was written in 1969. For more recent data, the reader should consult the sources in the Bibliographical Note.

Figure 1. Industrial Expansion (1900 = 100)*

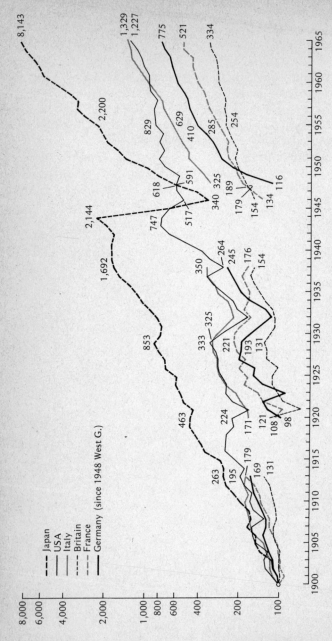

* Figures are index number of manufacturing production with the base year 1900 as 100. This graph was prepared by Yutaka Kitagawa.

SOURCE: Hyōe Ōuchi et al. (eds.), Nihon Keizai Zusetsu (The Japanese Economy Illustrated), 4th ed. (Tokyo: Iwanami, 1967), p. 7. Reprinted by permission.

sufficient explanation for an understanding of the characteristically Japanese mode of combining the two contrasting sides.

Notwithstanding various criticisms, Ruth Benedict's *The Chrysanthemum and the Sword* (1947),[2] one of the pioneer works in Japanese studies, is still helpful for an understanding of the two contrasting aspects of Japanese culture. Numerous academic studies about Japanese society have explored the exotic, inherent, peculiar aspects of the Japanese personality. The reader interested in pursuing this topic more deeply can begin with Benedict's work. But this present study will attempt to examine those features of Japanese society which have been basic to prewar, postwar, and contemporary Japan. Although such specific traditional attitudes as *on* and *giri* emphasized by Benedict are no longer very important, seemingly contradictory aspects of Japanese society still remain.

The two faces of Japanese society and their relationship are the most interesting problem to be analyzed here. Let me illustrate with a few examples which will indicate the combination of contradictions. The first example can be found in the building of skyscrapers. It is often said that the skyscrapers of today's Japan are designed by computers, but at the ground-breaking ceremony there is usually a Shintō ritual to pray for safety during the construction. The second example is the contrast between the increased production and consumption of TV sets and refrigerators (Japan now ranks second in the world in the number of both per 100 persons) and the lack of space in the average Japanese house for these appliances.

The production of TV sets and refrigerators in 1962 was 300 times that of 1953. In 1968 96.6 percent of households in urban areas and 96.3 percent of those in rural areas had TV sets. In the same year an average of 77.6 percent of the households in Japan had electric refrigerators and 84.8 percent had washing machines. At the same time, the average number of persons living in one room was 1.4, and the average number of persons per household was 4.05. According to the national census of 1965, the average space per person is approximately 6 *jō* (1 *jō* is 4.8 by 2.9 feet, the size of one of the straw mats which form the floor of a Japanese house). Therefore, in an ordinary household, the TV set, refrigerator and washing machine have to be accommodated in a very small living space. It is easy to imagine how crowded the rooms are. After the traditional evening bedding is spread on the floor, very often almost no extra space is left.

Today's housing conditions are not very different from those witnessed by R. P. Dore in 1951, when he wrote: "There are fifty-nine [couples out of 300 households] in Shitayama-cho, who live with children in one room."[3] It was reported that the workers of Yawata Iron and Steel, which recently combined with Fuji Iron and Steel to form the second largest steel company in the world, live in company houses of only two rooms (one of 6 *jō* mat size and the other of 3) but many of them have their own cars and can be considered privileged when compared with other workers, especially those in small and medium-sized enterprises. At certain periods it has been reported that in one of the Yawata Company's subcontracting factories, the workers put in a 16-hour day, including 8 hours overtime.[4]

Despite these difficult living conditions, the Japanese people work hard, produce and save a lot. When considering the "miraculous" development and the relatively unpleasant individual daily life, it is difficult to decide which is the cause and which the effect. It is, however, safe to say that there is a high degree of correlation between the two. As Benedict wrote, "the Japanese have been described in the most fantastic series of 'but also's' ever used for any nation of the world," and "all these contradictions . . . are the warp and woof of books on Japan."[5]

It is easy to add to the list of the contradictions found in Japanese society. For example, the contrast between the apparent strength and radical attitudes of labor and left-wing movements and their slight influence on the actual policy-making process, which lies in the hands of a more or less permanently entrenched conservative government. But it is my major task in the following chapters not simply to indicate such contradictions, but to explain how they have come about and analyze the way in which they are combined, and suggest, in the light of these contradictions, in what direction Japan is moving.

Part One
HISTORICAL PERSPECTIVE

2

Cultural Heritage and Westernization

Different Cultural Influences and National Homogeneity

Japan, separated from the mainland of Asia by the East China Sea, is distant enough to have escaped military invasion, but not so far away as to have been unaffected by cultural influence from China. Chinese culture, which brought with it the Buddhist culture of India, began to influence Japan as early as the sixth century. This continental culture, which was more advanced and developed than that found in the Japanese court, was actively adopted to add to the prestige of the ruling class. Even the governmental structure of China was imitated by the Japanese in an attempt to unify the country. The Chinese influence came through Korea, which is separated from Japan by a strait only 25 miles wide. Since then, Chinese and Buddhist influences have been so widespread that the ordinary people of present-day Japan are not usually conscious of their "foreignness," and they are often regarded as a part of the native Japanese culture.

The Japanese language, although it bears no family relationship to Chinese (its structure is similar to that of Korean, and has features in common with that of the Ural-Altaic languages), is written with the Chinese script, and a great part of its vocabulary is taken from Chinese. Chinese terms and Buddhist concepts have provided a framework for Japanese thought. For instance, the Western concept "freedom" cannot be rendered precisely into Japanese, because the Japanese word *jiyū*, which is the usual translation, has also been used in Con-

7

fucian and Buddhist contexts, and hence inevitably has a meaning somewhat different from "freedom."

During the sixteenth century, mainly through the Dutch and the Portuguese, Western culture came to Japan, but this influence ceased at the onset of Japan's period of isolation, which lasted from the early seventeenth to the mid-nineteenth century. In 1853, Commodore Perry came to Japan to force her to open the door to trade with Western countries. Japan had been almost completely isolated for two and a half centuries, and all through her premodern history she had neither experienced conquest by foreign powers nor endeavored to extend her influence abroad. The only exceptions were the unsuccessful Mongolian invasions of 1274 and 1281 and one ill-fated expedition to Korea in the 1590s.

Under these geographical and historical conditions, Japan has been able to digest foreign cultures gradually and integrate them into her own. It is difficult for us today to determine what features of Japanese culture are genuinely indigenous, because different cultural influences have been closely mixed with the native culture. Already in the seventh century, when Japan first established a certain degree of national unity, there was a fusion of Shintō, Buddhist, and Confucian elements. The combination can be seen in the seventeen articles of the constitution promulgated by Prince Shōtoku in 604, although there has been no academic agreement about which of the three elements was predominant. The Shintō element in the constitution reflected the social structure of the time, when the primitive clan system was still predominant; the Buddhist element, with its transcendental value orientation, was introduced in order to overcome the particularism reflected in the domination of various clans; and the Confucian element was a consequence of the introduction of the bureaucratic administrative system from China.

Although indeed some factions questioned Japan's adoption of Buddhism, the ruling elite decided upon the introduction and combination of different foreign cultures in order to strengthen its own position. The gradual filtering of foreign cultures via the elite down to the lower strata of society served to avoid the internal conflicts and disturbances that have usually resulted from foreign cultural influences. Despite the variety of foreign cultures that have influenced Japan, the nation as a whole has been able to maintain its homogeneity and identity.

Thus, there is a curious cultural syncretism in Japan: For example, a god enshrined according to Shintō beliefs was also regarded as a *Bodhisattva* (a Buddhist saint). Even in modern Japan, many people celebrate their wedding with a Shintō ceremony which centers on "purification"; behave in their social life in such a way as to conform to Confucian ethics that emphasize adjustment to this world (although the influence of Confucianism is much weaker since the war); and are buried according to Buddhist rites that reflect the Buddhist orientation toward the other world. Of course, this sort of syncretism has been possible only because of the modification or Japanese adaptation of foreign cultures, which will be discussed later. From the eleventh-century novel *The Tale of Genji* to the paintings and woodblock prints of Hokusai (1760–1849), the great cultural achievements of the Japanese cannot be said to have been due to a particular foreign influence; rather, they should all be regarded as products of "Japanese" culture.

Although academic discussions concerning the ethnic origin of the "Japanese" people continue, Japan has been an exceptionally homogeneous nation for a long time because of the cultural unification of different influences in a relatively isolated chain of small islands (with a total area approximately the same as that of California). One obvious example of the national homogeneity can be found by comparing the Japanese driving license with the American. On the latter are recorded color of hair, color of eyes, and sometimes even "racial extraction," none of which appear on a Japanese license. Almost all Japanese have black hair, brown eyes, and the same ethnic origin, and speak only Japanese.

Similarly, there has been no diversity of religion in Japan. Until the middle of the last century, almost all Japanese were Buddhists, partly because of the suppression of Christianity. Even today, more than 70 percent of Japanese are "Buddhists," although this does not imply that they are church-goers or even believers in Buddhism; it simply means that they will be buried according to Buddhist rites. Buddhism in Japan is, of course, a Japanized Buddhism different from the original. At least at the first stage, it was introduced into Japan in Chinese translations and hence was biased by the Chinese interpretation. Since then, Buddhism has been a kind of national religion, and has undergone much interpretation and development within Japan. Especially important was the great change in Japanese Buddhism in the thirteenth century, which Max Weber called a "reformation."[1] This "reformation" resulted in an increased emphasis on activities in this world. After the establishment of the Tokugawa shogunate, however, Buddhist temples became an administrative instrument of the government. It became obligatory to register one's name at a temple in order to prove one was not a Christian. Thus, although Buddhism prevailed in Japan, it sacrificed its beliefs and became part of the ritual custom of daily life.

Similar adjustment to Japanese social conditions can be found in the case of Confucianism too, which was propagated in Japan by the warrior class, whereas in China it was propagated by the literati. Even in the Tokugawa period, when the Chu Hsi interpretation of Confucian theory enjoyed the status of orthodoxy, Japanese Confucianism put more emphasis on practical ability than was the case in China, where simple memorization of the Confucian classics was all that was necessary to pass the examination for entry into the bureaucracy. In Japan, the absence of the Confucian examination system was an advantage, since it allowed the ruling elite to show a more flexible response to the need for rapid change.

Another legacy advantageous in allowing Japan to begin modernizing was her national unity. From the seventeenth century onward a semicentralized government existed, and by the beginning of the period of modernization about a hundred years ago, Japanese society already had a relatively high degree of national unity. During three hundred years of unified rule and peace there had been developments in communication, rudimentary scientific techniques, and education sufficient to begin the process of modernization. Japan also had far fewer regional differences than Germany, for example, where the states (Länder) had more independence than the regions of Japan, and where the process of modernization also started later than in other developed countries.[2] It was on this sociological basis that Japan was able to modernize herself rapidly through the unanimous efforts of all her people. The ruling elite possessed a strong awareness of Japanese technological and military inferiority in the face of Western demands for diplomatic and commercial relations, and was able to mobilize the people in a concentrated effort to meet these demands. This attempt to modernize was a focused, unifying national goal that will be discussed below.

"Escape from the East, Enter into the West"

As in the case of China, Japan passed through three different stages of response to the Western cultural impact: total rejection, partial acceptance, and full-scale Westernization. It was also common to both China and Japan that at the beginning of the period of partial acceptance, awareness of Asian military inferiority made it necessary for the political leaders to first introduce Western military technology before adopting other aspects of Western civilization. In Japan, however, reluctant partial acceptance was more rapidly replaced by full-scale Westernization than in other Asian countries, where there existed such socioreligious inflexibilities as Confucian dogmatism in China and the caste system in India.

Japanese leaders considered it necessary to establish a Western legal system as well as a Western frame of government in order to achieve revision of the unequal treaties with Western powers that forced Japan to accept a disadvantageous tariff rate and gave legal privileges to foreigners in Japan. The decision that there should be a broad range of Westernization was made more easily in Japan than in China, whose ruling elite tended to cling to Confucian belief in the superiority of "the Central Empire." Once the decision was made, Westernization took place first in the upper strata of society, and then filtered downward without being hindered by such sharp class distinctions as the caste system. Many Western features were adopted as a result of demands from discontented factions within the ruling elite, who espoused Western ideologies in an attempt to improve their own situation.

It was remarkable that within a few years Westernization became a national goal and was carried out rapidly and even with a considerable degree of popular enthusiasm. Not only Western military technology and a Western type of legal system, but all kinds of things Western, from clothes to the custom of eating beef and pork, which was prohibited in the Buddhist tradition, were considered to be symbols of "civilization and enlightenment," a fashionable term in the early 1870s.

During the two decades following the conservative ex-samurai rebellions, which had ended by 1877, the Japanese government devoted its efforts to the revision of the unequal treaties. Such efforts ranged from the promulgation of the Constitution of 1889 and the codification of the civil code and other Western types of laws, to the holding of fancy-dress balls attended by high officials and other distinguished people in the famous Rokumeikan in Tokyo, which had been specially built for Western-style social gatherings. Despite some resistance on the part of conservative nationalists, the slogan "Escape from the East, enter into the West" was commonly considered to indicate Japan's national goal.

Other factors that contributed to the rapid and virtually unopposed introduction of Western culture were the high degree of literacy and the national educational system. "By the time of the Restoration forty to fifty percent of all Japanese boys, and perhaps fifteen percent of girls were getting some formal schooling outside their homes."[3] After the establishment of the system of compulsory education in 1872, the proportion of those attending school increased rapidly and had reached almost 90 percent by the end of the century.

On this foundation it was possible to build a system of higher education. Especially important was the fact that even higher education was taught in Japanese, except for classes taught by a small number of Western teachers. Many Western books were translated into Japanese —for example, works by Jeremy Bentham, John Stuart Mill, Jean-Jacques Rousseau, and Herbert Spencer. The fact that Western science and literature were introduced by means of translations contributed to Japan's maintenance of national unity and identity in the face of rapid Westernization. Because of the strong national homogeneity and the near unanimity of the effort to Westernize, Japan was able to assimilate Western culture without a great deal of internal conflict or a crisis of identity.

After Japan's victories in the wars with China in 1894–1895 and with Russia in 1904–1905, the Japanese people had gained enough confidence to believe that their nation was already one of the great powers of the world. The increased self-confidence weakened the desire to "escape from the East," because it was thought that Japan had already been quite successful in achieving Westernization. At this point a new slogan emerged: "Fusion between the East and the West" —which was actually a demand that Japan assume the leadership of Asia. At the same time, this slogan reflected the internal need to reconcile traditional elements with Westernization, because the social diversity resulting from urbanization was threatening national homogeneity. Especially serious among the problems due to such diversity were peasant resentment of urbanization and labor problems resulting from industrialization.[4] Difficulties resulting from industrialization and urbanization, which were aggravated particularly by the depression of the 1930s, were considered by many Japanese to be traceable to Westernization.

Of course, blaming Westernization for these problems was partly the result of indoctrination by the governing elite, who wished to channel popular discontent into ultranationalism. The resentment among peasants toward urbanization and Westernization, expressed, for example, by military officers from rural areas at the time of the military coups in the 1930s, was one of the factors that led Japan into a catastrophic war in 1941.

After Japan's defeat in World War II and during the succeeding occupation, the fashionable dichotomization between feudal and modern was often identified with that between Japanese and Western. Popular enthusiasm for things Western revived as an acute reaction to the ultranationalism of the preceding years, when all personal happiness was sacrificed to the national cause. The revived Western influence, however, was different in two respects from that before the war. First, the influence of America replaced that of Germany, which had been predominant among Western cultures in terms of institutional as well as intellectual influence. Second, there was a new pattern of influence. Previously, the popular image of America had been formed by tales about industrious and serious-minded men such as Benjamin Franklin and men of high ideal and principle such as Abraham Lincoln. Now, for the first time, ordinary Japanese people were directly exposed to everyday Western behavior. For instance, the GI attitude toward life, exemplified by their expression "take it easy," made a vivid impression on the Japanese man in the street. The extreme contrast between the material affluence of the American armed forces and the near-starvation of the Japanese contributed to the change that took place in the Japanese view of their own country and of their former enemy.

Thus the old pattern of introduction of Western cultures changed: Foreign influence no longer necessarily came through the sociopolitical elite, nor did it gradually filter down from the upper to the lower strata of society. This change was one of the causes of the chaotic situation immediately after a war in which Japan had experienced defeat for the first time in her history, alone a sufficient reason for her cultural breakdown.

Far East or Far West

The peace treaty signed at San Francisco in 1951 gave Japan formal independence, but it was accompanied by the Japanese-American security treaty, which allowed the United States to continue to station troops in Japan. Dominant American influence during the occupation was followed by a reaction which is called "the reverse course." In the period of this reaction, a revival of Japanese customs (the tea ceremony, flower arrangement, and the wearing of Japanese clothes) appeared, together with political reaction against postwar reforms—for example, land reform, economic democratization, and constitutional revision.

"Independence" and the extremely rapid economic development that followed brought an increase in national self-confidence. This increase, however, did not ensure the success of the political reaction exemplified by the "reverse course" slogan. This was because the results of the postwar reforms had already taken root so deeply in daily life that the majority of Japanese did not want to see them destroyed. As such results are not felt to be simply imports from the West, it has become difficult even for the Rightists to reverse the democratic way of life and system of government by invoking nationalist sentiment.

The highly urbanized society of contemporary Japan provides an appropriate social basis for a Western type of civilization, although of course with some necessary modifications. For instance, Japan has in common with the developed countries of the West a high degree of consumption-orientation, in part created by advertising through the mass communications media. And present Japanese society may be described as "post-industrial," for the percentage of those who are engaged in tertiary industry (45.4 percent in 1967) is almost as high as in advanced Western countries.

In addition to the existence of phenomena obviously common to both Japan and Western societies, there are elements in Japanese society that have caused some of these phenomena to appear in an exaggerated form. One such element is the long tradition of group conformity, which, however, is not now part of a monolithic emperor system as it was before the war. The prewar unit of conformity was the nation, whereas today the units are multiple and fragmented. Although the old pattern of introducing Western cultures via the upper strata of the society changed after the war, this does not mean that each individual has come to respond to Western influence. Rather, there is continuity between the pre- and postwar patterns in that both have emphasized group conformity. All sorts of new fashions from the rest of the world, such as new styles in clothing from Paris and psychedelic art from the United States, have been introduced into Japan, and partly because of the tradition of conformity, have rapidly gained favor, at least with some groups. One of the reasons why durable consumer goods, such as television sets, have spread extremely rapidly is that group conformity puts pressure on the individual household.

These things can be seen at a glance. There are, however, some more important things hidden beneath the surface which are related to the question of why some Western phenomena appear in Japan in an exaggerated form. A residue of traditional attitudes was sometimes an accelerating factor for certain aspects of industrialization. For example, during the time of total war, the traditional residue, such as fanatical ultranationalism, was fully utilized to facilitate economic and political mobilization. Moreover, certain aspects of modern technology, such as the mass communications media, were highly developed and utilized under the militarist regime. Fanatical ultranationalism was not always a hindrance to the use of modern technology. The militarist regime, which appeared as one of the results of a particular type of rapid industrialization, made some defects of modern society extremely explicit.

It should be noted that the use of the contrasting terms "modern" and "traditional" should not always be taken to mean that the more a country is modernized, the fewer the traditional elements that remain. On the contrary, traditional elements sometimes contribute to rapid development and to its one-sided appearance.

It is sometimes said that Japan should be called part of the Far West rather than the Far East because she has so much in common with the West. It would be more appropriate to say that Japan is at the same time a part of both. Using both these terms is not necessarily contradictory. Under certain circumstances, the characteristics of Western mass society may be exaggerated by Eastern tradition. For instance, the traditional lack of inner-directed individualism strengthens the conformism of mass society. Similarly, traditional political indifference can easily be combined with mass apathy. Conformity and apathy, both intensified by traditional elements, were the basis for unanimous support under the militarist regime.

I do not mean to imply that another militarist regime will make its appearance in Japan, but simply that the curious combination of traditional and Western elements in Japanese society significantly distorts certain aspects of the latter. We can see some of these distortions in Japan's "miraculous" economic development and the "misery" created by the social problems that accompany it.

3

"Enrich the Country and Strengthen the Military"

Industrialization with a Dual Structure

The bitter experience of having been forced to sign unequal treaties with Western countries made Japanese leaders of the Meiji period feel it necessary to "enrich the country and strengthen the military," a popular slogan in early modern Japan. Because Japan began her Industrial Revolution more than a century later than some Western countries, the government made every effort to promote industrialization in order to catch up. For example, various advantages were given to emerging industries. In the beginning, the government itself operated factories such as spinning mills and munitions plants. Later, many of these factories were sold to private businessmen at relatively low prices, although the important munitions industry remained in the hands of the government. Telegraphic and mail services and railways, established by the government in the 1870s, were prerequisites for industrialization.

One important characteristic of Japanese industrialization, in contrast with that of other late-developing countries, is that the capital to be invested for industrialization was practically all obtained internally without recourse to foreign aid. This, of course, made it easier for Japan to maintain her independence. The major source of finance for initial investment was the heavy land tax. The rate was 3 percent of the land value, but the value was decided by the government. Landowners shifted the burden of the tax to their tenants, who often had to forfeit about two-thirds of their harvest as rent.

While in England it was the enclosure movement which created the rural exodus that provided factory workers, in Japan the wretched condition of the peasants, whose sons and daughters were often forced by economic necessity to leave their villages for jobs in factories, played this role. But Japanese peasants did not leave the countryside for good, for they usually maintained close relationships with their home villages through family ties. Very often, a girl who worked in a spinning mill, the daughter of a poor peasant, became ill and had to return home; or a second son who worked in a factory had to ask his father or brother for support when he lost his job. Thus, lack of social security was compensated for by family or extended family ties, which also saved expense on the part of industry. This situation prevailed until 1945.

The existence of close ties between workers and their families in the home villages not only made recruitment and maintenance of cheap labor easier, but also provided Japan's rapid industrialization with a safety valve, chiefly psychological, that inhibited serious class conflict between employers and employees. The likelihood of class conflict was also reduced by a paternalistic management policy designed to make workers feel that the factory was a quasi-family.

In the process of rapid industrialization artificially promoted from above, the dual structure of the economy was apparent: privileged industry on the one hand and underprivileged agriculture on the other. A similar dualism later arose between large enterprises and smaller ones, the combination of which has been an important characteristic of the Japanese economy up to the present day. Workers in large factories have been relatively privileged in terms of both wages and job security compared with those in smaller enterprises. Management in large enterprises has been highly developed, whereas the organization of small enterprises is not very different from that of household industries.

Subcontracts between larger and smaller factories have formed an inseparable link between the two. The real significance of the term "dual" is not simply that the two different sectors coexist, but that there is a close interrelationship between the two, so that neither can exist without the other. The existence of a dual structure in the Japanese economy has been an advantage as far as rapid industrialization is concerned, in the sense that large enterprises can expand their business by increasing the number of their subcontracts without worrying very much about depressions, to which they can partially adjust by decreasing the number of subcontracts.

However, this dual structure inevitably produced a condition that has been disadvantageous for industrialization. Low purchasing power, accompanied by high production stimulated by expenditures on munitions and heavy industry, required that Japan should find markets abroad. In the prewar period, the principal method of acquiring markets was the threat of violence.

The high rate of military expenditures also contributed to rapid industrialization. Government investment and special financial aid such as subsidies for the munitions industry, which included such heavy industries as shipbuilding, was an effective stimulus to industrialization as a whole. At the same time, the fiscal burden of military expenditures, which reached 47.2 percent of the annual budget in 1936, inhibited balanced economic development.

After the war, investment in the munitions industry ceased, and this contributed to the rapid recovery of the Japanese economy, because a vast amount of capital was freed for highly productive investment projects. Despite the tendency toward "affluence" of the society as a whole, the dual structure still remains, in the sense that a considerable gap continues to exist between large enterprises and small and medium-sized enterprises. Even in 1966, workers in factories with less than 20 employees received about half the wages of workers in factories with more than 1,000 workers. Although this gap between the two has been decreasing recently (in 1968, workers in factories with less than 100 employees received 60–80 percent of wages of workers in factories with more than 1,000 workers), if we consider the other advantages of workers in large factories, such as company housing and job security, the difference is still great. And it is not very likely that the gap will be abolished in the near future, because the dual structure has become an essential characteristic of the Japanese economy. The secret of the "miraculous" postwar development can be found partly in this dual structure, as will be explained in more detail later.

Conflicts Resulting from Industrialization

This dual structure inevitably resulted in increased sociopsychological tension between the privileged and underprivileged sectors of society during the process of industrialization. Resentment against industrialization was conspicuous among the peasants from the beginning. They believed, with sufficient reason, that their interests were being sacrificed for the sake of rapid industrialization. Attempts were made to pacify them, but without success, and they continued to feel disgruntled. Their discontent often turned to nationalism or expansionism, because they tended to identify industrialization, which was, in their view, the cause of their difficulties, with Westernization, and hence to find their psychological compensation in the expansion of the Japanese Empire, which seemed to them to be an anti-Western venture.

Up to the beginning of this century, the majority of Diet (national legislature) members represented the interests of landowners, whose influence was predominant in the constituencies. Hence they advocated reduction of the land tax. Serious conflicts occasionally took place between the government, which was in favor of industrialization, and the Diet, which claimed that government policy was sacrificing agrarian interests.

The conflicts between the Diet and the government, which reflected the conflicts between rural and urban interests, gradually disappeared, partly because of a decrease in the need for government aid for industrialization, and partly because of an increase in the number of Diet members who represented, at least in some degree, the growing business interests. Then another conflict resulting from industrialization appeared: that between industrialists and wage earners. This conflict was first reflected in the emergence of labor disputes and unions, and then, to a limited extent, in the Diet after the first general election under universal manhood suffrage in 1928. Under the emperor system, however, the left-wing ideological movement in general, and the Marxist movement in particular, found it difficult to acquire legitimacy. Hence it was extremely difficult to organize mass movements, and labor movements could not become militant enough to bring about any radical change in the political situation. Instead, partly because of rigorous suppression by the police, labor movements turned their energies to support of the expansionist policy, finding in it a psychological projection of their feelings of dissatisfaction.

A more common form of dissatisfaction found in this dual-structured society was that felt by underprivileged people as a whole—for example, the feelings of the old middle class, whose status was declining with the development of industrialization. Small landowners, shopkeepers, and factory owners, their foremen and artisans, who belonged to this category, were influential in local community life. In showing antipathy toward the elite of society, toward intellectualism, and toward industrialization, all of which were considered to be results of Westernization, they represented popular feeling in an extreme form. To use a military analogy, the role of such local leaders can be compared with that of noncommissioned officers who form the link between officers and men. The content of nationalistic indoctrination, understood by members of the elite in a relatively flexible way, became extremely rigid when interpreted by these mediators.

One reason why resentment among underprivileged people formed a nationwide social basis for ultranationalism can be found in the homogeneity of Japan, which produced a desire to maintain national harmony by avoiding the internal conflicts resulting from industrialization. Many people, including many members of the elite, feared that once this harmony was disrupted, there would be a complete breakdown of national unity. Not simply because of the resentment among underprivileged people, but also because of the elite's own fear of this possible disruption, extreme sensitivity toward divisiveness within society prevailed throughout the nation.

This fear seemed to have had sufficient foundation in the 1930s, when the critical economic situation was considered to be a danger to national harmony. The feeling of solidarity had been based upon actual community life in villages where people worked together, cooperating in irrigating, transplanting, and harvesting the rice. Despite rapid industrialization, the absolute number of those engaged in agriculture was almost the same in 1930 as in 1868, and in fact they still formed a majority of the total population. The strong agrarian flavor of Japanese ultranationalism can thus be partly explained by the peasants' resentment against industrialization, identified by them with Westernization.

Wherever rapid industrialization is carried out with government initiative playing a major role, it is almost inevitable that there is, to a certain extent, a socioeconomic lag between the industrialized sector and the rest of society. The direction in which the discontent of the latter can be channeled differs from country to country. It was a historical irony that national homogeneity made it easy for Japan to assimilate Western culture with high degree of unanimity, and then, when serious internal conflict arose as a result of industrialization, served to intensify anti-Western feeling. That feeling became so intense during World War II that the radio stopped broadcasting music by Western composers except for that of Germans and Italians. The Pacific war, which was called "the Great East Asian War" at the time, was justified in Japan as being fought for "the Greater East Asian Co-Prosperity Sphere" against Western imperialism.

In the postwar period, conflicts resulting from industrialization, such as urban problems, still remain, and will be discussed in a later chapter.

Party Government and the Militarist Regime

These conflicts resulting from the Japanese way of industrialization were closely related to the various social phenomena which I have indicated. These various conflicts and the related social phenomena can partly explain the establishment of a militarist regime between the late 1930s and the early 1940s. The problem of why party government was replaced by a militarist regime is a complex one. To say that the system of party government was overthrown by a militarist clique is an oversimplification, since weaknesses within the system itself contributed to its downfall. Let us consider the political consequences of the process of industrialization.

As industrialization proceeded, a Western type of government gradually took root, and political parties emerged. The increased influence of the business world, together with popular demands for a more democratic government, led in 1913 to the breakdown of the oligarchic administration headed by General Katsura, one of the *genrō* (elder statesmen). It was on this occasion that a mass movement with a certain degree of influence appeared on the political scene for the first time in Japanese history. This popular movement, led by party leaders and called the "Taishō democracy" movement (Taishō is the name of the period 1912–1926), resulted in the passage of the Universal (Manhood) Suffrage Law in 1925. Although an attempt by a small group of industrialists to establish a political party ultimately failed, the business world as a whole, led by the *zaibatsu* (financial cliques) exercised a powerful influence on the political parties through the provision of financial assistance.

This close relationship between parties and business bred corruption which was eventually exposed to the public and attracted a good deal of popular attention. Especially after the introduction of "universal" suffrage, political parties that lacked a mass organization had to appeal more directly to the new larger electorate. Emotional slogans, pamphlets, and posters came to be used to appeal to the mass of the people. Among the most effective weapons employed in election campaigns were accusations of corruption and lack of patriotism; one party would accuse its opponents of not "conducting themselves properly as subjects of the Emperor." This method of exposé and accusation adopted by all major parties undermined confidence in party government in general. Thus the parties dug their own graves, and invited the formation of a "supra-party" cabinet in 1932 which "transcended" party control and which put an end to party government in prewar Japan.[1]

Against this social background, such antiparty ventures on the part of the militarists as the assassination of the prime minister in 1932 gained a certain amount of popular support. This was because the mass of the people resented the corruption of the party cabinets and saw in the expansionist policy of the militarists a hope that some attention would now be paid to their interests. Anti-Western feeling combined with dislike of industrialization created distrust of parliamentary government, which was considered, like industrialization, to be a Western phenomenon and therefore unsuited to Japan. The influence of Fascist ideology, together with the idea of "the decline of the West" formulated by Oswald Spengler, intensified this distrust. In particular, people in rural areas, who constituted 76 percent of the total population in 1930,[2] turned for an effective solution toward the army officers whose "constituencies," as they were called, were the farming villages.

After the failure of a military coup attempted by some of these officers in 1936, there was no longer an important open threat of physical force on the domestic scene. On the other hand, the entire regime took on a Fascist hue through institutionalization of the anti-Western feelings of the nation. At the same time, businessmen cooperated in organizing the economy for total war because of their own interest in increased profits from munitions production. The interests of large industries and the resentment of industrialization felt by the mass of the people, contradictory though they were, contributed to the establishment of a militarist regime.

Maintenance of national harmony was one of the chief concerns of the political leaders, who thought it necessary to buttress integration by operating on the traditional desire for consensus existing in the rural communities. A link between the central government and local communities was established by the bureaucracy through neighborhood associations or agricultural organizations. Thus the political parties lost their raison d'être as a link between the government and the people, and in 1940 dissolved themselves into a monistic, semi-governmental organization called the Imperial Rule Assistance Association, where "harmonious consensus" replaced majority rule. The strong fear of the breakdown of homogeneity caused by industrialization and urbanization now became extremely institutionalized. For instance, people were forced not only psychologically, but also at times by social sanctions such as ostracism, or by a warning from IRAA officials, to conform with others even in their manner of dress.

A brief explanation should be given here of the emperor system, which continued to play an important role until 1945. During the course of the Meiji Restoration of 1868, the continuity of the imperial tradition, which had functioned as the symbolic center of the nation, served as the focus of the Restoration Movement and was used to supplant the old regime. At the beginning of Japan's modernization, the existence of the emperor, who had for centuries been separated from the actual power center, the shōgunal government, provided Japan with a symbol of flexible change and at the same time one of identity and continuity.

In the process of consolidation of the new government, the position of the emperor was defined in the Meiji Constitution promulgated in 1889. His position was, however, ambiguous in the sense that he was neither "the king in parliament," nor an absolute monarch. Although in terms of legal institutions the emperor system may be described as a sort of constitutional monarchy, the imperial prerogatives, especially that of supreme command of the army and navy, ensured, in fact, that the emperor was completely free from the control of the Diet. This priority of the military over the civil government was, of course, one of the reasons for the emergence of a militarist regime.

More important, however, was the extra-institutional role of the emperor as a symbol of national conformity. Because his function was symbolic, no one could know the real will of the emperor, who was completely free from any responsibility to the Diet. Rightists or militarists often said that they were doing what the emperor really wanted. Since Japanese patriotism, identified with loyalty to the emperor, did not have any transcendental or universalistic orientation beyond the imperial family, the emperor came to be an ethnocentric symbol.

Thus, once national conformity, stimulated by the feeling of national danger, took on a right-wing appearance, it became difficult for dissenters to make their voices heard not simply because of their fear of suppression by the police, but because of social pressures supported by the threat of ostracism. As has been said, even the tendency toward diversification of society was used to intensify national conformity.

An intensified national conformity deprived Japan of flexibility of response, since even her leaders felt themselves to be bound by it. To put it more extremely, it deprived them of the awareness of the necessity for sensitive decision-making. For example, the prime minister, Hideki Tōjō, believed the decision to go to war was inevitable. In all probability, he was not conscious of making a decision; he thought he was merely following the natural trend of events. The emperor, to whom Tōjō thought he was loyal, once told one of his favorite senior statesmen confidentially, "I wish the war would come to an end soon."[3] Most Japanese, including the emperor and the prime minister, thought of the war as if it were a natural phenomenon, brought about by the world situation and internal national conformity. The militarist regime could therefore not be overthrown by political forces within the country; instead it had to be destroyed by the military might of the Allied Powers.

4

American Occupation

Impact of the Occupation

Military defeat, which Japan experienced in 1945 for the first time in her history, and the succeeding occupation by the Allied Forces were a fatal shock to the old regime. Since the Allied Powers desired a change in the whole structure of Japanese society, which was, in their view, the cause of Japan's total commitment to war, occupation policy was directed not only toward the disarmament of Japan, but also toward her demilitarization and democratization. The drastic changes ordered by the occupation authorities meant that the period of the occupation (1945–1952) was an epoch-making one. So drastic were the changes made during the early part of the occupation that it has become common for the Japanese to regard the immediate postwar period as entirely distinct from both the prewar and postoccupation periods.

The initial policies of the occupation were aimed at the abolition of the major instruments of the old power structure, for instance, the Privy Council, the House of Peers, the imperial army and navy, and the special political police. An attack was also launched on the advocates of ultranationalism. The wide-ranging political purge designed to expel nationalists and militarists from public office and the abolition of ultranationalist organizations were part of this policy.[1]

In addition to policies whose results were almost immediately obvious, there were others such as the disestablishment of Shintō, the prohibition of the teaching of ultranationalistic history and "ethics," and the alteration of the contents of textbooks for compulsory education, that helped to produce long-term changes in value orientation.

The influence on the social structure of reforms carried out during the initial stages of the occupation was of prime importance. A partial attempt at land reform had been made by some members of the government during the war, but it was not until after 1945 that this was accomplished, at the initiative partly of the government and partly of the occupation authorities. Its most far-reaching effect was a drastic change in the structure of rural society. The hierarchical relationship between landowners and tenants was abolished; owner-farmers, who had become independent of the former (often absentee) landowners, were now free to improve agricultural productivity and reap the reward for their initiative. Land reform, the purge of ultranationalists, and the basic change in the family system (the abolition of the extended family as a legal entity) resulting from the revision of the civil code together destroyed the social basis of the old order.

Economic democratization was accomplished in several progressive steps: First, the dissolution of *zaibatsu* holding companies; then the revival of labor unions, whose activities were protected by legislation (for example, the Labor Union Law) and encouraged by the policies of the occupation authorities. Despite difficult postwar conditions, labor unions were often successful in improving the economic lot of their members. In this sense, the vicious circle that existed in the dual structure of the prewar economy, which was characterized by cheap labor and relatively weak purchasing power, was at least partially broken. This was particularly so in the case of developed industries that could afford to meet labor union demands. Ironically enough, labor disputes, which often resulted in an ostensible defeat for the employer, in the long run created advantageous conditions for industrial expansion by increasing consumer purchasing power.

The constitution promulgated in 1947 included a declaration of popular sovereignty (Preamble and Article 1), a renunciation of war (Article 9), a guarantee of fundamental human rights (Articles 11–40), and a commitment to parliamentary government (Articles 41f). Although these principles were really meant as guidelines for the reorientation of Japan, it was a considerable time before they took root in Japanese life because they were widely regarded as a "gift" from the occupation authorities and therefore as something alien to Japan.

It is, obviously, a contradiction in terms to "force" someone to be free.[2] However close to the ideal the occupation policy may have been, real freedom could not arise spontaneously under the occupation. It was therefore natural that there should be, immediately after the end of the occupation, a reaction against the postwar reforms. Since then, the Japanese people have themselves reevaluated the results of those reforms.

Other factors also limited the effects of the reforms. For one thing, the occupation was undertaken almost exclusively by the agents of a single country, the United States, although in the name of the Allied Forces. After the beginning of the cold war, it became difficult for the United States and the Soviet Union to reach agreement on the direction and scope of Allied activity in Japan. In fact, as tension increased, occupation policy came to be decided by American national interests rather than by consensus among the Allied Forces. The policy of demilitarization and democratization was replaced by one of rearmament and "de-purge" in order to strengthen Japan as a new ally of the United States in Asia. The outbreak of the Korean War in 1950 marked a clear turning point in this respect, although a gradual movement in this direction can be traced back to 1947.

The effects of the reforms were also weakened by the fact that they were carried out by the Japanese government. The occupation of Japan differed from that of Germany, where each occupying country ruled the zone allotted to it and there was no central German government. In Japan, the occupation authorities ruled indirectly through the government. The sector of society that underwent least change during the occupation was the bureaucracy, because it was the agent through which occupation policy was executed. It was often reported that members of the bureaucracy attempted to impede the working of the reforms ordered by the occupation authorities.

Historical Continuity and Discontinuity

Despite the strong impact of the occupation, the effects of the reforms ordered by the occupation authorities were limited by these factors, so that the question may be raised of how much historical discontinuity exists, on balance, between the pre- and postoccupation periods. It is almost impossible, and probably unhelpful, to answer this question quantitatively, since historical continuity and discontinuity should be examined from various points of view. Furthermore, in no sphere was there an example of *absolute* historical discontinuity between the pre- and postoccupation periods. Some aspects of the relationship between historical continuity and discontinuity are illustrated by the following three examples.

First of all, historical discontinuity is most marked in the case of the emperor system. As has been said, this system was deprived of its legal standing as well as of its ideological integrity through occupation policy. After the reforms, the emperor could neither be supreme commander of the imperial army and navy, nor the head of the bureaucracy, which in fact integrated the whole society. The position of the emperor as the ideological center on which national conformity and feelings of loyalty were exclusively focused through ultranationalistic indoctrination was changed by rescinding the Imperial Rescript on Education originally issued in 1890 and by various other reforms in education.

This seemingly total destruction of the emperor system as a power structure as well as an ideological system was, however, accompanied by historical continuity, in that the fragmented parts of the society formerly integrated by the emperor system still survived with some of the characteristics of the prewar period—for example, strong group conformity composed of closed we-consciousness.

Something should be said here briefly about the continuity and discontinuity between group structure in the pre- and postoccupation periods. There has been a clear change in the sense that the relationship among members has become less hierarchical. Hierarchical relationships between the landowner and his tenants and between the main family and its branch families have virtually disappeared in rural communities. A similar change can be found in factories, where hierarchical relationships between foremen or senior workers and rank-and-file workers have become much less important than before.

Although this change was mostly due to the influence of the postwar reforms, a gradual decline of the influence of the hierarchical structure could already be observed even before the end of the war. For instance, after the economic crisis of the early 1930s, the government attempted to reconstruct the village order by encouraging the growth of a middle class of owner-farmers rather than large (especially absentee) landowners. The interests of the latter were also circumscribed during the war in order to increase productivity. Because of technological innovation, among factory workers, too, seniority in terms of length of training had been lessening in importance compared with actual technical ability. In this sense, there is a historical continuity between the pre- and postoccupation periods.

More clearly, continuity exists in that feelings of solidarity and conformity among villagers, as well as among workers in the same factory, are still strong despite the changes in the hierarchical structure. Indeed, it can be said that, in one sense, group conformity has become stronger partly *because* of the disappearance of hierarchical relationships.[3] Although the social context is different from that of before the war, conformity among the inhabitants of a village or among workers in a factory has survived and still plays an important role. For instance, in the villages conformity is the basis for agricultural cooperatives, whose smallest unit is the hamlet and which in 1957 comprised more than 99 percent of farming families. In the factories, conformity is one of the basic sources of industriousness and hence of high productivity. At the same time, it buttresses the cooperative spirit of the labor unions, which in Japan are based on the individual company.[4]

The third example of parallel continuity and discontinuity can be seen in the continuing importance of the family system and the familistic principle of social structure (or to put it more broadly, the importance of personal relationships) and the simultaneous tendency toward depersonalization. This change again was chiefly due to the postwar reforms, including the revision of the civil code and the ideological breakdown of the emperor system. Both filial piety and feelings of personal loyalty to the emperor decreased remarkably after the defeat. On the other hand, the tendency toward depersonalization can be observed even in the prewar period, as industrialization developed. Inevitably, depersonalization took place particularly rapidly during the war because of the necessity for mobilizing all human resources; for instance, city children were forced to leave their homes for the countryside in order to escape the bombing, and girls had to work in munitions factories, thus breaking the old tradition that women should stay at home. These facts, of course, resulted in the impairment of the old family system.

The doctrine of the "family-state" which regarded the state as a huge family with the emperor at its head was abolished, and the Imperial Rescript of January 1, 1946 denied the emperor's divinity. Loyalty to the emperor was discredited because a war fought in his name had ended in defeat. The abolition of the family-state doctrine along with other reforms resulted in snapping the link between loyalty to the emperor and filial piety, and in the disappearance of popular belief in the hereditary charisma of the emperor.[5]

This change, however, did not result in the emergence of an inner-directed individualism completely emancipated from traditional values. Rather, many Japanese, deprived of the old ideological consistency, looked for something with which they could identify, and on which they could depend. The fragmented social groups that had formerly been integrated into the old emperor system became the object of this identification and dependence. This is partly the reason why group conformity is still as strong as or even stronger than before the war, even though "groupism" in fragmented sectors of society no longer has any link with a national value system.

The emperor himself is now nothing more than the object of sentimental attachment among the older generation. Among younger people, the Crown Prince and Princess are popular for much the same reasons as are movie stars. Without a focal point for national integrity, groupism readily becomes the source of factional conflict in various sectors of society—for example, in political parties, labor unions and other organizations. This point will be discussed later.

Legacy of the Occupation

At the end of the occupation in 1952, Japan became legally independent, and new developments took place. The political process could now operate without open interference from outside. The emergence of two major parties (as a result of amalgamations among the conservative parties on the one hand and the socialist parties on the other) and the development of oligopoly in business (in the absence of the restraints formerly imposed by the occupation authorities on economic concentration) are examples of these developments. There was a parallel trend in the growth in size and number of certain important organized pressure groups, such as the Japan Federation of Employers Associations, which had been forbidden during the first stage of the occupation. The dominance of the two major parties has recently been impaired by the tendency toward a multiparty system, although the country has remained under the same continuous semipermanent government of the conservative party. But despite these surface changes during the postoccupation period, the legacy of the occupation remains influential.

One part of this legacy is that the results of the postwar reforms have begun to take root. Some of the major principles of the new constitution, such as popular sovereignty, pacifism, and the guarantee of fundamental human rights, have come to be regarded in the popular mind as basic principles of government. The conservative government has therefore not felt able to carry out its intention of revising the constitution so as to modify these principles.

The principle of popular sovereignty has become something more than a "gift": It has taken root to such an extent that, for example, when political corruption was revealed in the Tokyo Metropolitan Assembly, it contributed to the defeat of the government party candidate in the gubernatorial election for the first time since the war. The hold that the principle of pacifism has on the popular mind has often been indicated by the response to the war in Vietnam and Japan's commitment to it (more specifically, to the problem of American military bases). The Japanese people are not always conscious of pacifism and popular sovereignty as *principles;* rather, what they experience is pacifist sentiment and a desire for what they regard as a proper democratic process. Nevertheless, these feelings may be the embryo of a genuine pacifism and a real commitment to the principle of popular sovereignty.

The fundamental human rights, too, have become something which the mass of the people now believe in. Those who were formerly interested primarily in maintaining social harmony and in avoiding conflict even when their fundamental human rights were jeopardized have now become aware of the necessity of defending them. Although, as in the case of the land distributed to farmers by the land reform, fundamental human rights may also have been regarded as something "given" to the people, it has now become almost inconceivable that limits should be placed on the rights they actually exercise. Particularly among the young people of Japan, it is now natural to be sensitive to any threat to their fundamental rights. This sensitivity is not always firmly based on a consciousness of "rights" as distinguished from vested interests, but again, it may be the harbinger of a true commitment in the future.

If this is the brighter side of the legacy of the occupation, there is also a darker side. As has been said, occupation policy was mostly executed by the Japanese bureaucracy, whose influence was an established fact long before that of other political forces such as the political parties and continued even after the end of the occupation. Despite the constitutional principle of parliamentary government, the bureaucracy has become an agent not only of policy execution, but also of policy-making. There is a close connection between the bureaucracy and the government party; for example, almost a third of the conservative Diet members began their careers in the bureaucracy.

A further reason for this ascendancy of the bureaucracy can be found in another legacy of the occupation—the lack of creative leadership by able statesmen among the Diet members. From the beginning of modern Japan, the government has been successful in recruiting competent bureaucrats from various sectors of society through the national educational system and through civil service examinations.[6] On the other hand, Japan has never been successful in recruiting capable political leaders from within the political parties. Not only in the prewar period but also up to the present, the majority of the heads of major political parties have come from the bureaucracy, which before the war included the military bureaucracy. And the occupation authorities ordered no drastic changes in the bureaucracy. They made the important policy decisions themselves, and then had them implemented through the Japanese bureaucracy, so that there was little need for Japanese political leaders who could make important policy decisions. Thus the lack of competent party leaders is in part the legacy of the occupation, and in part the historical tradition of modern Japan.

The scarcity of Japanese initiatives in world affairs and the ready acquiescence of the Japanese government in American foreign policy are also a residue of the government's attitudes under the occupation. It may be that the contrast between relatively developed popular attitudes on the mass level and relatively weak leadership by party leaders is one of the most important legacies of the occupation. As time passes, the memory of the occupation is becoming weaker. Many young people, of course, do not remember it at all. Thus, Japanese society retains some legacies of the occupation without, on the whole, being aware of the fact.

Part Two

BASIC ELEMENTS
OF
JAPANESE SOCIETY

5

Values, Norms, and Education

Conformity and Competition

When Japan surrendered in 1945, many Americans thought that there would be strong resistance to the occupation because of the fanatical patriotism they had encountered among Japanese soldiers during the war. What happened in fact was that the Japanese people quietly accepted American occupation. How could this rapid change in Japanese attitudes have come about? Part of the explanation is that one of the most important means used by the Japanese people to achieve their national goal, whatever it may be, is conformity. Conformism in Japan, however, is not simply passive obedience. Conformism based on passive obedience would tend to result in immobilism, and it would be difficult, if Japanese conformism were of this kind, to explain Japan's success in developing herself so rapidly. The question naturally arises about what sort of value-orientation has made Japan more dynamic in "modernization" than other Asian countries.[1]

Traditional Chinese and Japanese cultures had in common the element of Confucianism, which emphasized the importance of conformity to the social order. In the case of Japan, however, conformity did not mean that attitudes were static, or that there was a reluctance to change the existing situation. Rather, it implied conformity to the *changing* situation. For instance, at the beginning of the modernization of Japan, the people, led by the governing elite, responded rapidly and almost unanimously to the need for Westernization.

When people are unanimously changing in the same direction, opposition to change is failure to conform: Once members of the same group start running in the same direction, not to run as fast as the others is disrupting to group conformity. Because the content of loyalty to the emperor was not clear, the only way one could prove one's loyalty was to do something obviously more "loyal" or at least to avoid doing anything that might be considered less loyal than the others. For instance, wearing *kimono* (Japanese clothes) with long sleeves was usual among young ladies until the last war, but when the war reached its most serious stage, it was considered disloyal or unpatriotic to wear such clothing because it was expensive and unsuitable for doing work. In this case, failure to relinquish traditional clothing was considered to be inappropriate behavior.

In the case of ideas too, when large numbers of people were being converted to fanatical patriotism, those who did not change their views were considered to be traitors. Dr. Tatsukichi Minobe, who advocated a theory in which the emperor was regarded as an organ of the state, was the most influential scholar in public law between the beginning of this century and the early 1930s. But after the Rightist attack on his theory in the early 1930s, it came to be considered heresy.

Closely related to this characteristic is another factor that helps to make Japanese conformity dynamic: competition. There may be competition within a conformity or between conformities. When we say that Japanese conformity is conformity not to the static order but to the changing situation, one might well ask who decides the direction and speed of the change. It is very difficult to answer this question, because the change is not necessarily wished for by anyone, but may be rather the result of competition. For instance, the dissolution of the various political parties and labor unions was not simply the result of threats from the Rightists, but was at least partly the result of competition in loyalty among these bodies themselves. They actually competed with each other in dissolving themselves in the hope that the earlier they did so, the stronger their position would be in the Imperial Rule Assistance Association that was to be established. Competition in loyalty among organizations helped to propel Japan toward ultranationalism.

This sort of nationwide competition in loyalty to the emperor no longer exists. The same structure of competition, however, still prevails in fragmented segments of society. Among company employees, for instance, a strong sense of identity with the company and conformity to its goals is accompanied by a sense of competition both externally with other companies and internally in loyalty to their own company. It is easy to see that strong conformity among workers in the same company correlates with their inclination to compete with other companies in the same field. Thus, conformity not only does not stand in the way of competition, but actually contributes to it.

But more important here is the fact that competition among the workers themselves is not destructive of conformity, since it is competition in loyalty to the company. In this way, competition results in unanimity of effort. This sort of competition is not an indication of individualism in the strict sense; it is rather the obverse of group conformity: The orientation of the members of the group is not toward individual achievement, but toward merit acquired by individual contribution to the goal of the group.

The tradition of group conformity in Japan probably originated in the communal life of rice-growing villages, in which it was necessary for the villagers to cooperate closely and in which the daily life of individual farmers was usually absorbed in the life of the village.[2] After the establishment of a nation-state, the government tried to spread this group conformity throughout society by means of education. At the same time, the traditional warrior ethic, which emphasized the importance of dynamic action rather than passive adjustment to the status quo, was included to form an important part of the national morality. Thus there emerged a combination of the principles of conformity and competition very different from the passivity of, for example, traditional India.

In the process of industrialization, the traditional village structure was threatened by the tendency toward urbanization. The tradition of group conformity was, however, transplanted to urban life in the sense that conformity among workers in the same factory was, to a certain extent, similar to that in rural communities. Despite, or even because of, the changes in situation that led to a decrease of solidarity in rural life, there was a strong feeling of nostalgia for the "good old days." This nostalgia, which existed in urban as well as rural areas because many workers felt insecure without close personal ties, buttressed the family-state idea—the Japanese "Fascist" ideology with an agrarian flavor.

Since the destruction of the integral nationalism in World War II, there has been no single center to which every Japanese devotes himself, but there still remains the need for a group with which people can identify, on which they can depend, and to which they can devote themselves. The feeling of insecurity of the isolated individual in mass society, which has arisen in all highly industrialized societies, has strengthened this popular need. The fact that in Japan the inner-directed personality did not develop has also increased this need. Thus loyalty to various groups prevails, even though it no longer has a national focal center. This group conformity, together with the principle of competition, is one of the elements in her society that are most important to an explanation of Japan's "miraculous" postwar economic development.

Religious Feeling

This devotion to the group has something in common with religious feeling. The brave deaths of Japanese soldiers on the battlefield were a reflection of their belief in the divinity of the emperor, the center of the nation. It is probably not true, however, to say that the Japanese people's devotion to the emperor or their self-sacrifice for the nation was due to their belief in Shintō. Shintō has no sacred book, and it does not embody belief in one God. According to Shintō, "gods" exist, but there is no belief in a single transcendental deity. This lack of belief in the transcendental is one of the most important characteristics of indigenous Japanese culture.

Buddhism, which was introduced into Japan in about the sixth century, included a belief in the transcendental, but not in a single God. In Japan, Buddhist belief was modified so that the transcendental element was linked with order in this world. The assertion of an interdependence between Buddhist belief and political order has been a salient characteristic of Japanese Buddhism.

Despite the importance of the revival of the transcendental element in the thirteenth century, Buddhism, as it became more and more deeply rooted in society, lost much of its spiritual significance and became primarily the source of the rituals of daily life, such as funerals. The Japanese people have almost always had a this-worldly cast of mind, and no process of secularization was necessary to modernize the nation; the acceptance of Darwinian theory, for example, was not hindered by any religious belief. This was also true of the introduction of most Western ideas. In the early modern period many Japanese intellectuals used the Darwinian theory and other positivistic Western theories to criticize Christianity.

At the same time, it would be misleading to say that the Japanese people are completely without religious sentiment and only interested in the existing social situation. There has normally been something beyond the existing situation to which people have devoted themselves and which has provided them with a goal. For instance, the familism prevalent in traditional Japanese society included something beyond the existing family order. In merchant families, the eldest son was expected to succeed to the position of head of the family, but if he had no ability, a successor of greater talent was sometimes recruited by adoption for the sake of "the name of the family," which was above and beyond the existing family order.

Similarly, Japanese nationalism demanded that the existing situation be changed in conformity with a national goal. Nationalists were able to propose various social changes in the name of the nation. Although this is no doubt true of nationalism everywhere, a special characteristic of Japanese nationalism is that it was entwined with worship of the emperor. How was it possible to reconcile nationalism as a goal and the particular will of the emperor? The authority of the emperor was considered to have originated in the will of the ancestors of the imperial family, by which the will of the individual emperor was limited. However, the real will of the ancestors of the imperial family, whose lineage was traced back as far as "the Sun Goddess Amaterasu," could not be known. Since the will of the emperor was thus by its nature unknowable, anyone could invoke it in support of a particular course of action. In actuality, however, the will of the emperor was not completely separated from the secular order, but was realized by the governing elite through the bureaucracy. Thus a substitute for the transcendental was delicately linked with the secular order.

Devotion to the nation no longer plays any important role in Japanese life. Since Japan's defeat, people have had little interest in a national goal, although the 1964 Tokyo Olympics and Expo '70 were exceptions for which many people worked hard and in which many felt pride. Generally, people are more interested in their own happiness and that of their families than in the destiny of the nation.

Devotion to emperor and nation, however, has left a double legacy: First, devotion to nation and emperor has been fragmented and now exists in the form of devotion to various groups, such as the companies or unions. Such devotion does not conflict with a person's desire for personal happiness, because in his view, working hard for the company will make him prosperous. Not a few companies send their employees to Zen Buddhist temples for periods of meditation or to the Self-Defense Force (the Japanese army) for periods of character-building discipline in order to strengthen their devotion. Many employees themselves think this is a good idea, but the majority of them add that, although they think it a good thing to learn discipline in the Self-Defense Force, they do not like war.

Second, there exists a strong feeling of nostalgia for the dedication of prewar days. Complaints are widely heard among older people about the lack of discipline among the young in present-day Japan. And even among young people themselves, there is some hunger for discipline and dedication, a tendency illustrated by the popularity of novels that deal with the devotion and self-sacrifice of young army officers at the time of the military coup of 1936 and thereafter. This popularity does not mean that many people are interested in the ultra-nationalistic cause to which the heroes of those novels dedicated themselves, but is rather an indication of the readers' approval of the esthetic values, such as "purity," which they find in the militarists' behavior.

Although it is said that more than 70 percent of the total population of Japan consider themselves to be Buddhists, this does not mean they are devout believers in Buddhism. The majority of Japanese are indifferent to all organized religion. Sometimes, however, esthetic values act as a substitute for religious values, in the sense that devotion to something, whatever it may be, is considered to be "pure" behavior and hence highly approved. Even among the students of the Zengakuren (National Federation of Student Organizations), we may observe a sort of hunger for dedication.

The recent development of new religious sects, of which the Sōka Gakkai, with believers in 6 million households, is the most important, can also be explained, at least partly, in terms of the same tendency. Many of these sects enforce a strict discipline and demand complete devotion from their believers. One of the reasons for their success is that they have organized mostly the underdogs of society, those who previously had no organization to depend on, and have provided them an object with which they can identify and to which they can devote themselves. The various strictly disciplined group activities satisfy the members' hunger for dedication, and the group conformity gives them a feeling of security.

One important characteristic of devotion among Japanese is that it is not usually directed toward something transcendental, but rather toward something connected with the group. Even among the new religious sects, this seems to be the case, although the believers themselves think they believe in a transcendental religious value. A new quasi-Christian sect called Genrikenkyūkai (The Society for the Study of Fundamental Truth) is worth mentioning here: The devotion of the members, many of whom were students, was so fanatical that their parents had to form a group to "rescue" them from the organization, because they left home and refused to return.

Christians, who compose 0.7 percent of the total population (approximately one-third are Roman Catholics and almost all the rest are Protestants), hold, of course, the similar beliefs as the same denominations in Western countries, although during the war most of them made concessions to the emperor system and accepted the ultranationalistic ideology.

One concern common to all Japanese, whatever their religious beliefs, and which in many ways resembles a religious feeling, is their concern for peace. It is illustrated by surveys of public opinion which always show a large majority opposed to any kind of war. For instance, a nationwide public opinion poll conducted in 1965 indicated that 75 percent of those who were asked opposed the American bombing of North Vietnam, whereas only 4 percent supported it.[3] Popular concern for peace is so intense that the government has been unable to carry out its wish to revise the "Peace" Constitution of 1947, one clause of which renounces war "as a sovereign right of the nation and the threat or use of force as means of settling international disputes." Although it may be an overstatement to say that the majority of Japanese believe in absolute pacifism, it is true that pacifist sentiment is prevalent throughout the nation.

Because of the atomic bombing of Hiroshima and Nagasaki, whose victims are still dying of diseases due to the bombs, the Japanese people are extremely sensitive to the danger of nuclear warfare and to any danger from radioactivity.[4] Their strong reactions to nuclear tests by any country and to the visits of American nuclear submarines to Japanese ports, which has sometimes resulted in increased radioactivity, are examples of this sensitivity.

Education and Upbringing

Upbringing in general and school education in particular undoubtedly play the most important roles in maintaining the norms and values of a society. In Japan, school education has had particular importance because churches have played only a negligible role as agents of socialization. Another factor that increased the importance of formal education was the government's use of the school as a channel of indoctrination. Furthermore, a high degree of vertical social mobility through education has produced the phenomenon called in Japan "education fever."

For white collar workers and the majority of manual workers, employment is normally "for life" (that is to say, the employee usually remains with the same employer from the time he leaves the school or university until he retires). It is therefore very important for the white collar worker to be graduated from a "good" university. The competition to enter a comparatively small number of prestigious universities is so great that roughly half of those who are successful in passing the entrance examination for the Tokyo University, for instance, have already tried more than once. This situation has created a large number of *yobikō*, private schools that coach students for the university entrance examinations. The competition, in fact, is so fierce that it is difficult to get into the best of the *yobikō*.

Since graduation from one of the dozen or so most prestigious universities almost guarantees an excellent job, parents are eager to send their children to a good high school so that they have the best possible chance of getting into these universities. As a result, many parents are deeply concerned about which elementary school they should send their children to; and it has even been reported that there are schools which coach children for the entrance examinations for the best kindergartens. It is not at all rare for even elementary school children to have personal instruction at home or to be sent to an informal school after regular school hours.

The interest of parents is usually focused so narrowly on examinations that many of them tend to forget the "unexaminable" content of education. This tendency often results in a lack of interest in moral education at home. On the other hand, because of the historical tradition of the importance of formal education, and because of their heavy reliance on school, not a few parents ask their children's teachers to strengthen moral training, which they "cannot" give at home. This dependence on school for moral education has made it easier for the Ministry of Education, the government organ with strong control over the national educational system, to revive "ethics" as part of the compulsory curriculum.

One of the most important characteristics of moral education in Japan has been the result of strong political influence. Because moral education and education in Japanese history played an important part in the growth of ultranationalism, the occupation authorities ordered this sort of teaching abolished. After the end of the occupation in 1952, moral education was revived in the schools despite the opposition of various liberal political groups who feared increased nationalism. The government has also attempted, with gradual success, to bring about a change in the content of the Japanese history taught in school.

The changes in education that took place immediately after the war have resulted in a conflict of values between the different generations. There is a particularly wide gulf between those who were educated before the end of the war and those educated since. Loyalty to the emperor and to the head of the family, which formed the core of moral education in the prewar period, have lost their influence on the younger generation. The conflict of values between generations, which is seen everywhere, has been deepened in Japan by the drastic changes in education and in the value system as a whole which took place during the occupation period.

Furthermore, the radicalism of many students, which is a common phenomenon all over the world, has been intensified by these differences in values. In addition, "education fever" has resulted in the overprotection of students by their parents, which sometimes results in a widening of the gulf between the values of students and those of other sectors of society. Even in the process of the formation of the individual's values, there is a distinct discontinuity before and after graduation from the university. Although this discontinuity occurs, to a certain extent, everywhere, it has been especially marked in Japan because of the traditional strength of group conformity. It often happens that a student who has engaged in fierce and often violent political battles while at the university becomes overnight a docile and loyal employee.

Up to the university level, there is a high degree of equality of opportunity, in the sense that, given the ability to pass the entrance examination, it is possible to get into a good university regardless of family background. Of course, the student's family must be able to afford to allow him to concentrate on preparation for the entrance examination, and also to pay the university tuition fees, but these are very low in the case of the national universities ($33.33 per year). There are more than 800 universities and colleges, with more than a million students, but the standing of individual universities varies greatly; and since the kind of job a student is able to get when he graduates depends largely on the reputation of his university, he is able to foresee his future fairly accurately.

When a student graduates and joins a company or enters the civil service, his life is already mapped out, since lifetime employment is the norm and there is little horizontal mobility. Of course, there is still competition for promotion, but it is confined within a framework of promotion by seniority. The seniority rule is still rigidly observed in many organizations. For example, when the highest permanent official of a government ministry resigns, his successor is chosen from among a few officials of equal seniority. If those who are not selected for the post were to remain, the seniority structure of the ministry would be unbalanced, so it is not uncommon for them to be given new jobs in some other government organization. The fact that the competition is confined within a framework does not necessarily mean that it causes less psychological tension than school and university examinations. Competition within limits may be all the more intense because of the limits.

There is a clear contrast between the free competition in terms of achievement up to the university level on the one hand and the inflexibility and lack of horizontal mobility after graduation on the other. Naturally, the two different worlds have different values and attitudes. The continuity between the two lies in the fact that the period up to the university level is regarded as a preparatory stage for the later career. Because of this link between the two stages of life, the values of the later stage can influence those of the earlier, and thus cause a conflict of values among young people. This conflict of values, and the psychological tension resulting from the pressure of entrance examinations, have intensified the problems of youth normally found in many developed societies, such as juvenile delinquency and suicide. It can be observed that the suicide rate is high, compared with other societies, in late adolescence, that period of life into which "the opportunities for mobility are highly compressed,"[5] and in the period after retirement.

Since the chaotic period immediately after the end of the war, stratification has occurred in the various sectors of society. The result has been the establishment of a stable—indeed, many would say stagnant—order. If we examine the differences in income among employees, it may seem to be relatively small compared with many other societies,[6] but this is not the major reason for the feeling of stagnation. Rather, it is the discontent concerning the future: Each person's future is so clearly calculable (for instance, when one reaches a certain age, one's income and position are determined by seniority) that one's imagination, dreams, and hopes seem futile.

It is easy to imagine the discontent of those who feel alienated from this tightly bureaucratized established order, and of those who are in the lowest strata. Not only psychologically, but sometimes also physically, many isolated people have been affected adversely by vast entrenched organizations, for example, by the air and water pollution caused by large factories. So far not much has been done to solve this sort of problem because the traditional lack of voluntary associations in Japan has made it difficult for those affected to organize so that their protests will have an impact. Recently, however, numerous small civic groups have emerged to give expression to such demands. The emergence of these groups is partly the result of changes in values and education since the defeat, and of recent distrust of the socialist parties and other established "progressive" organizations such as labor unions, and partly the result of the fact that housewives, who are most active in such groups, have more spare time because of the introduction of labor-saving devices into the home.

Youth organizations, women's organizations, and other adult organizations for social education have been developing since the end of the war. There are now more than 8,000 Citizens' Public Halls in which the various activities of such organizations are carried on. The Social Education Law was revised in 1959 so that the government could subsidize organizations for social education (which was previously prohibited in order to prevent government interference). Those who belong to large organizations or firms have no interest in using public facilities, because they are satisfied with the group activities within their own organization. The facilities provided by the firm for entertainment, hobbies, and so forth are often better than the public facilities. Most of those who are outside these large organizations, such as retired people, housewives, and people working in small enterprises, are attracted by the activities of the government-subsidized bodies. These organizations for "social education" are not party organs, but they can be used indirectly for political purposes. For instance, during an election campaign, a folk song club for old and middle-aged people may be used as a machine to collect bloc votes for a government party candidate.

In sum, polarization is taking place between truly voluntary civic groups, which are concerned with social or political issues, and those which are subsidized by the government and mostly concerned with hobbies and other leisure activities. The latter either increase political apathy or are indirectly influenced by the government and the conservative party which has been in power for so long.

6

Family and Community

Family

The old Japanese term *ie*, which could mean family, house, or home, also had connotations which those terms do not have. One of the most important characteristics of the *ie* was its emphasis on the unbroken family line. The *ie* also was related to "a set of rules about how members were to behave." In accordance with this set of values, "one person had to be chosen as family head and all other members were to relate to each other depending on their position within the *ie*."[1] The *ie* was characterized by the following features: (1) It was an "extended family" (that is, a main family and its branches), and there existed a hierarchical relationship among the main and the branch families. (2) Each family within the *ie* was patriarchal in structure. (3) Members of the family owed obedience to the head of the family, and the branch families owed allegiance to the main family. In return, the main family provided a kind of "social security" for the branch families in time of need, and the head of each family provided similar security for the members of his family. (4) The solidarity of the *ie*, and filial piety, institutionalized in the hierarchical structure of the *ie*, were the ideological basis for the family-state idea, a concept which regarded the state as a single family with the emperor as its head, the relationship between ruler and subject being analogous to that between father and son.

When the abolition of the emperor system, both as power structure and as ideology, was ordered by the occupation authorities, the family-state idea broke down. The civil code was revised so that "parental rights" and the "rights of the head of the family" were no longer embodied in the law. The revision of the civil code also resulted in the new system of equal rights of inheritance among children, which replaced the old tradition of primogeniture and thus in principle destroyed the privileged position of the first son as successor to the head of the family. In addition to these legal reforms, land reform, which created a class of more or less equal independent farmers, deprived the main family of the resources to control and protect the branch families. The increase in social mobility associated with urbanization also weakened the solidarity of the extended family, whose members originally lived in the same rural community.

Nowadays the prevailing type of family is the nuclear family (a family comprising either a married couple alone or a married couple and their children, excluding the couple's parents, brothers and sisters, and other relatives) resembling that of Western societies. This is shown by the fact that the average number of persons in a household in 1965 was 4.05. With urbanization there is also the tendency for the family to abandon the role of basic unit of production, a role which it has always played in agrarian societies. Today, roughly 80 percent of farming families also engage in some business other than agriculture: For example, the husband may work either part-time or full-time in a factory. There is a noticeable tendency for the family to become a unit of consumption rather than of production.

Although the term *maihōmushugi* (love of family life; literally, "my-home-ism") is common in present-day Japan, the idea it refers to differs from the old familism in the following ways. First of all, the new "my-home-ism" is not linked to a national ideology. Its influence is, rather, centrifugal, tending to divert the attention of the individual from national concerns to the happiness of his own family, and is antagonistic, or at least indifferent, to any integrated nationalism. Second, "home" in this case means the nuclear family and has nothing to do with the extended family or with the family line. Third, "my home" does not include the hierarchical relationships which existed in the *ie*, nor is it concerned with differences in status among family members or between main and branch families. Last, the major interest of the members of the family is more in consumption than in production, which is true of many developed societies.

These changes of attitude in family life do "not necessarily imply anything which can be called a 'triumph of individualism,'" although "the notion of the 'transcendental' unity of the family group across the generations is greatly weakened."[2] A wife is not obliged to be obedient to her husband as the head of the family. The honor and interest of the family line in the abstract has ceased "to be a value of any motivating importance."[3] Both husbands and wives, however, still work hard for their families.

Public opinion poll questions asking "From which goals do you derive the most satisfaction?" always show a majority answering "working and living for husband or wife, children and self" or "for a happy family life," whereas "working and living for the emperor" or "for the nation" obtain only a negligible percentage.[4] In this sense, it may be said that "attitudes of collectivity-orientation can still survive in a new form."[5] For instance, when a child is studying for examinations, the whole family is deeply concerned, and tries to be as quiet as possible so that the child will have the best possible conditions for studying. Marriages arranged by the parents are still not rare, and young people themselves are often in favor of arranged marriages, taking the realistic view that the system may produce a more suitable partner than their own unguided choice.

The arranged marriage of today is not the same as it was before the war, when very often the couple saw each other only once before the wedding ceremony. Nowadays, the *miai* (a formal meeting between a young man and a young woman with a view to their possible future marriage, usually in the presence of their parents and of a couple acting as go-betweens) is regarded as the beginning of a period during which the young people will go out together and get to know each other before deciding, for themselves, whether to marry. Cases in which parents arrange their daughter's marriage without consulting her, or against her will, which were common before the war, are now very rare.

When a couple has children, their interest, particularly that of the mother, tends to be concentrated on the children. The mother generally devotes herself to their upbringing. Even in the case of a family of the new middle class, which represents in many ways the most radical departure from tradition, it is reported that the mother provides her children with continuous attention.[6] For instance, she usually sleeps with the child, and she carries it on her back when she goes out shopping. This intimate relationship and close physical contact between mother and child is one of the special characteristics of the Japanese family. The intimate relationship continues to exist until the children reach late adolescence, although occasionally they revolt because they feel the close tie with their parents to be a burden. Many students who come to take the university entrance examinations are accompanied by their mothers or even by both parents.

Undoubtedly, this way of rearing children, and the strong sense of solidarity among members of the family, are not favorable conditions for establishing individualistic attitudes. Despite the changes in attitudes in family life since the postwar reforms, and perhaps largely because of the disappearance of hierarchical relationships within the family, the dependence on the family of its members has been increased.

The high degree of interdependence of members of the family signified by the term "my-home-ism," however, does not necessarily mean that the husband gives priority to family life and neglects the rest of his social life. On the contrary, ordinary workers, including white collar workers, leave home early in the morning and do not return until late in the evening, since they often work beyond the regular hours and after work customarily spend some time in social contact with fellow workers or customers. This time spent drinking with companions is partly relaxation, but at the same time partly work, in the sense that it is necessary to maintain good personal relations with these people. In addition, it takes time, often more than an hour in an extremely crowded train, for an employee to get home from his place of work, so it is rare for him to be in time for an evening meal with his children. Sometimes it happens that a father sees his children only when they are asleep. At any rate, the ordinary middle-class husband has little time to spare for his family. Naturally, he leaves the running of the home to his wife; and while the husband depends on his wife in this way, the wife feels that the harder he works, the better his, and therefore her, future will be.

The ordinary housewife realizes that her husband's hard work promises a better future, but psychologically, she has to put up with long hours of solitude. The decrease in the amount of time spent on housekeeping, the result of the introduction of such durable consumer goods as washing machines, has made the housewife's loneliness even more intense. Left alone for long periods, she often tries to alleviate her discontent by lavishing attention on her children. "Education fever" and the overprotection of children are the results. Sometimes the discontented wife tries to keep her husband at home with his family by complaining that he works too hard.

With this sort of situation in mind, many companies expend a great deal of effort not only on intensifying the employee's own sense of identification with the company, but also on getting his family to identify. For instance, the slogan "my company, my home," frequently used in company newsletters, suggests a desire to turn the solidarity of the family to the company's use. Many companies have special programs, for example, sports days, for the entertainment of employees' families. When an employee's child starts school, the president of the company may give the child a box of pencils to commemorate the occasion. Although there is little chance of the new familism, or more precisely "my-home-ism," being used to strengthen an integrated nationalism, there is still much scope for it to be used to strengthen conformity in fragmented social groups such as companies. It sometimes happens that an employee's son works in the same factory, but even if this is not the case, the families of company employees tend to feel they are also part of the company when they make use of the company's recreational facilities, for example, the company hostels at the seaside and in the mountains.

Generally, the family in contemporary Japan is highly urbanized, but originally there were noticeable differences between urban and rural families. Of course the latter represented the indigenous characteristics of *ie*. *Ie* was, in fact, the basic unit of the rural community.

Rural Community

In every society, the rural community as a fundamental social group plays an important role in the formation of the social nature of the members because of its position as a primary group characterized by personal contact and cooperation among its members. This is even more true in the case of Japan, since the rural community has long been regarded as the social basis of national homogeneity and solidarity. In the process of modernization up to the end of the war, the family, the rural community, and the nation formed three progressively larger groups that were regarded as being of the same kind. In the nationalistic ideology, as well as in terms of social structure, the rural community was a microcosm of the emperor system. The concept of "peace in the hamlet" (which will be explained later) reinforced conformity throughout the nation and was the prototype of that Japanese attitude which can be characterized by a clear contrast between morality among ingroup members and morality vis-à-vis outgroup members (*Binnenmoral* and *Aussenmoral*, to use Max Weber's terminology). Strong ingroup consciousness creates a contrast between peaceful and harmonious attitudes within the group and hostile and sometimes even inhuman attitudes toward people outside the group.

Group conformity within the rural community originated in the life style of the traditional rice-growing village, which necessitated continuous cooperation among the villagers. For instance, they depended on the same river for irrigation of their fields and on the same common land for the collection of firewood and fertilizer material. The villagers had to work together at those times when much collective manpower was needed—at the transplanting and harvesting of the rice, the construction and repair of the roads necessary for cultivation. They also helped each other at weddings and funerals, and, indeed, whenever help was needed.

This daily cooperation was considered to be "good morals and manners," but the fact that cooperation took place does not mean that the villagers were all of the same social status. In fact, there was clear differentiation of status among them. For example, hierarchical relationships existed between main family and branch families and between landowner and tenants. The relationship of tenant and landowner was felt to be a quasifamilistic father-son relationship. Thus the two principles of hierarchical relationship and horizontal cooperation coexisted, sometimes supplementing each other and sometimes conflicting with each other. So far as the relationships among villagers could be plausibly explained by analogy with the family structure, the two principles were not mutually contradictory, since a quasi-father-son relationship between landowner and tenants did not conflict with the custom of cooperation among the villagers, who regarded themselves as being, in a sense, members of the same family.

Actually, however, the collective work of the village often benefited those who owned a great deal of land, although the large landowner did not make much use of the common land, which was mostly used by the poor peasants. When the relationship between landowners and tenants became depersonalized—for example, when the landlord became an absentee and lost his daily contact with his tenants—solidarity and cooperation among the villagers tended to be in opposition to the hierarchical relationship. The tenant movement that gained momentum in the 1920s was one indication of this tendency. This movement in turn made landowners feel it would be better to deal with tenant disputes through legal procedures rather than in the traditional manner. Sometimes they became less paternalistic, and even those landowners who had remained in the village left to become absentee landowners. Particularly after the economic crisis of 1929, which had a serious impact on agriculture, antagonism between large landowners and tenants became fierce. The government decided to reform the structure of the village by encouraging relatively small working landowners and independent farmers, even though it meant some concessions on the part of the absentee landowners. There was thus a tendency to put more emphasis on solidarity than on the hierarchical village structure.

Land reform, partly planned by the Japanese government and partly ordered by the occupation authorities, has had a similar, but more drastic, effect. Paradoxically enough, as R. P. Dore points out, on the one hand the abolition of hierarchical relationships due to land reform resulted in the creation of "independent" farmers, but on the other hand, "as the land reform has also strengthened the solidarity of the hamlet, it has increased the constraint on individual choice exercised by the hamlet community, increased the pressure on the individual to conform, and increased the demands made on the individual to sink a part of his individuality in the group."[7]

Even now examples have been reported of the unanimous recommendation by the hamlet (*buraku*, subdivision of the *mura* or village) of a candidate for the village assembly. At the time of the election campaign, strong constraint is sometimes exercised on the hamlet; it may even be picketed at night in order to prevent influence from outside and maintain the bloc vote. As late as 1952, the family of a girl who sent a letter to a newspaper exposing illegal actions taken by her neighbors to obtain bloc votes for a government party candidate for the Upper House was ostracized and forced to leave the village because she had "put the village to shame."[8]

As a result of the introduction of chemical fertilizers and agricultural machinery, the need for cooperation among the villagers has been decreasing. Irrigation, however, continues to be an important matter, to be decided upon by the hamlet or the village as a community. The use of machines for cultivation is also limited in the first place because there are so many small scattered pieces of land (the average amount of land owned by a farming family is roughly 2 acres), and in the second place because the land is often unsuitable, since it is terraced, for the use of large tractors.

Furthermore, although it may seem paradoxical, the weakness of local autonomy has intensified the constraint of the hamlet on the individual. Until the end of the last war there was a long tradition of lack of autonomy in rural communities, which were tightly controlled by the central government. For instance, the village head was not directly elected by the villagers, but appointed on the nomination of the village assembly by the prefectural governor, who was appointed by the central government. As a result of postwar reforms, autonomy was "given" to local administrative units down to the village level so that almost all public officials are now elected by the villagers.

Autonomy remains weak, however, because the financial resources of the village are limited. Because of the relative poverty of farmers, who are of course much better off than in prewar days but still far behind industrial workers, the village has to depend on financial aid from the central government, such as agricultural subsidies. As a result of urbanization, the rural areas tend to be forgotten and financial aid for them has been decreasing. The more limited the resources, the stronger the competition among the villages for a larger share. An analogy can be made with a hot dry summer, when, because there is less water available for irrigation, conflicts among villages using water from the same river become more serious. These conflicts, of course, intensify solidarity within the group. In fact, the chief reason why the people of a hamlet are eager to elect a member of the village assembly by casting the hamlet's votes as a bloc is their feeling that otherwise their interests would be neglected in the welter of competition among the various hamlets in the assembly.

Another important factor that has contributed to the maintenance of solidarity in the hamlet and the village is the role played by the agricultural cooperatives, which in 1958 included 99.5 percent of farming families in Japan. The smallest unit of the cooperatives is usually the "neighborhood association," which is a semi-official sub-organization of the village administration. The neighborhood association in the hamlet is modeled on the five-household group of the Tokugawa period, although the number of households included now is much more than five—sometimes as many as twenty. The cooperative is a multifunctional organization in the sense that it plays the roles of bank, supermarket, provider of chemical fertilizer and other agricultural commodities, and buyer and seller of rice and other products.

As the number of those who are engaged in businesses other than agriculture in the village or the hamlet increases, the importance of the role played by the agricultural cooperative decreases, and hence the importance of the role of its smallest units, the hamlet and the neighborhood association, also declines. However, the villagers as consumers, whether they are farmers or not, are still under the constraint of the village and the hamlet. In the late 1950s, I was told by a farmer in a famous rice-growing area that it was less efficient for him to own his own cultivator than for him and his neighbors to share a better one, but that it was necessary to have one because all the others had them. The same can now be said about vacuum cleaners and washing machines and other appliances. This situation will persist, despite the influence of urbanization on rural communities, as long as daily contact among villagers continues to be as close as it is now, although of course the interest of the villagers will be directed more toward consumption than production.

Urban Problems

Significantly, in Japan urban communities have much less communal life than in Western societies, partly because of the lack of a historical tradition of free cities. In fact, formerly, many people who had come from the villages to live in urban areas had closer contact with their main families or relatives in their home villages than with their neighbors in the cities. Today, few city dwellers still maintain close contact with their home villages, but this does not mean that they have closer contact with their urban neighbors. The employees of large companies (and frequently their families too) are so deeply involved in their companies that they have no wish for close contact with their neighbors. Often, they do not even know what kind of people their neighbors are.

Only among people of the old middle class, such as shopkeepers, who have lived and worked in the same place for generations, has there been a solidarity at all like that of the rural community.[9] An instance of this sort of solidarity is that shops in the same street will often decide to hold their special sales on the same day. The number and importance of such shops, however, have been decreasing as a result of the emergence of supermarkets.

A weakening of the sense of solidarity among long-established town dwellers on the one hand, and the rapid expansion of the cities, which encourages newcomers, on the other hand, naturally result in a decrease in the residents' concern with local issues. Usually, the percentage of the electorate that actually votes in urban areas is several points lower than in rural constituencies, where it is a little over 80 percent. This does not necessarily mean that people in the villages are more politically aware than city dwellers. Probably, the solidarity of the village or hamlet tends to make the villagers feel obliged to vote. Although it can be said that people in urban areas have been freed from the constraints of the traditional community, this emancipation has not necessarily resulted in the emergence of independent, responsible political behavior. Rather, the lack of public interest tends to hamper improvement of the situation in the cities. Because of this disinterest among city dwellers, the situation has reached near-chaos in extremely overpopulated cities such as Tokyo, whose average density of population is 12,300 persons per square kilometer (in some boroughs it is more than 30,000).

Thus, the hardships of city life have increased, and few remedies have been provided. One example of these hardships is the lack of public parks. In Japan, there are 2.1 square meters per person of park land, and there are only fourteen cities in which there are more than 6 square meters (the highest figure is 68 square meters). Many cities in Japan have less than 0.3 square meters, whereas Washington has 45.2, and New York 11.9 square meters. In 1965 roughly two-thirds of the old city area of Tokyo had no sewers, and 401 cities in Japan had no sewers at all.[10]

Among the various urban problems, the most serious are housing and transport. In Tokyo, according to 1965 statistics, 549,100 houses were needed to replace very old houses (which were 5,600 in number) and to relieve overcrowding. (A dwelling is "overcrowded" if two persons have less than 15 square meters of floor space, or four persons have less than 20 square meters; in 1965 there were 436,600 such households.) Because public housing plans lag behind the rapidly increasing need, it is often necessary to make dozens of applications for public housing if one is unlucky in the lottery by which selection is made.

In order to rent a house or buy building land within their means, people must look to the suburbs. This tendency makes traffic conditions worse. The rush hour trains carrying people from the suburbs to the center of the city are so crowded that at the major stations there are special "pushers" whose job is to pack as many people as possible onto the trains. It is estimated that two hours' travel under these conditions uses up 409.2 calories. Eight hours' office work uses up 740.0 calories, so that those people who spend an hour or more traveling from their homes to their jobs use up more than half as much energy in traveling as they do in actual work.

The increase in the number of cars, which reached 101 per thousand persons in 1968 (in the United States the figure is 510), does nothing to solve this problem, since it takes more time to travel by car than by train. The principal result is an increase in road accidents. In 1966, there were 1.08 casualties per thousand vehicles in Japan and 0.56 casualties per thousand vehicles in the United States. The number of persons killed in road accidents in Japan reached 14,256 in 1968 (this figure doubled within ten years). The chief reason for these high figures is that streets are narrow and often have no sidewalks, so that pedestrians are particularly vulnerable. Roads occupy 12 percent of the area of Tokyo and 9 percent of the area of Osaka, whereas in New York the figure is 35 percent, and in Washington 43 percent.

The poverty of city planning in Japan reflects the lack of interest in urban problems among city dwellers. Recently, however, the situation has become so serious that problems such as housing, over-burdened transport, road accidents, smog, and noise have forced themselves on the consciousness of the public. Small civic organizations have emerged to tackle some of these problems, and although they are few in number and their direct influence is not very great, they have contributed to a growth in public concern. It is probable that one of the reasons for the election as Governor of Tokyo of Dr. Ryōkichi Minobe, who was supported by the Socialist and Communist parties, by many civic groups and by many housewives, was the emergent demand for a solution to those problems which had been long neglected under conservative governors. The severe Tokyo smog problem is the reason why one of the most popular slogans used in

Dr. Minobe's election campaign was "A blue sky for Tokyo!"

Dangers to public health caused by certain sorts of industries, notably petrochemicals, have become a focus of concern for the people of the afflicted areas. There has already been some successful resistance: For example, in Mishima City a popular movement succeeded in preventing an oil conversion plant from being built in the city. It is too early to conclude from isolated examples of this sort that there has been an emergence of the civic consciousness Japan has lacked, and that urban problems will be solved as a result; but the hardships caused by these problems are now approaching a point beyond which they will become insupportable, and something must be done immediately to remedy the present situation.

7

Organizations and Institutions

General Characteristics

Before describing the various contemporary organizations, I would like to deal with the general characteristics of organizations in Japan stemming from her historical tradition. First of all, voluntary associations are not a part of this tradition. Under the Tokugawa feudal regime, there was, generally speaking, no right of association, although there were some exceptions such as guilds, which were permitted under special charters. The restriction of freedom of association was the case everywhere under feudal regimes, but more so in Japan because there were no medieval free cities, except for Sakai in western Japan.

The Constitution of 1889 guaranteed the right of association, although with reservations. Under this constitution, various ostensibly voluntary associations were established at the instigation of the government. For instance, the forerunner of today's Chamber of Commerce and Industry was organized with the help of the government, which wanted a body through which it could consult the merchants and industrialists on the problem of customs duties. The chamber was subsidized by the government, and even when it later became more independent, it retained some legal privileges and at the same time remained under legal regulation. The same can be said of the agricultural organizations, which were created by law with a stronger initiative on the part of the government than in the case of business organizations.

Even political parties were originally organized by former government leaders or by ex-bureaucrats. The parties developed thereafter to such an extent that the party cabinet became customary in the early decades of this century. Labor unions emerged too, and eventually became a force that had to be reckoned with in fixing wages and working conditions.

When the Imperial Rule Assistance Association (IRAA)[1] was formed in 1940, almost all organizations, including political parties and labor unions, dissolved themselves in order to join it. One of the reasons why the IRAA was able to absorb all existing organizations can be found in the competition among the leaders of these organizations who were forced by widespread nationalistic sentiment to try to exhibit a stronger nationalism and loyalty to the emperor than competing organizations.

Another, more important, explanation is that the relatively weak position of organizations vis-à-vis the government strongly encouraged each organization to compete with the others to gain greater favor with the government. Historical evidence indicates that each union or party thought that if it did not take a stronger initiative than the other unions or parties in the formation of the IRAA, the others would have more influence in the new organization in terms of financial advantage and distribution of posts. The dissolving of various organizations into the IRAA, therefore, meant that the members of these organizations did not join the IRAA as *individuals*. The consequence was that the IRAA had no organic unity and was essentially a conglomeration of elements from different organizations. This, of course, resulted in internal difficulties arising from factional conflicts.

Since the emperor system no longer exists, recurrence of this phenomenon is unlikely. There are still, however, some remnants of the traditional attitudes of organizations toward the government. This can be seen particularly among weaker organizations, such as those which have obtained subsidies from the government (for example, agricultural organizations and associations of small and medium-sized enterprises).

A second characteristic can be found in the traditional Japanese attitude toward organizations, which considers them to be organic unities. For instance, members of agricultural cooperatives usually think it natural to be members of the village cooperative simply because they were born in the village. The same can be said of labor unions, in the sense that workers feel it natural to join the union that has been formed in the factory in which they work. (Japanese unions are organized on a company basis, all the employees of a particular company belonging to the same union regardless of trade or craft).

Closely related to this traditional attitude is the tendency for each organization to be all-embracing, to take in all potential members in a certain sphere, such as a village or a factory. Of course, physical proximity of members, their living or working together, is not a feature of every organization, certainly not of the more functional organizations such as business associations. However, the tendency to be all-embracing has characterized all Japanese organizations to a greater or lesser degree.

Leaders of organizations have favored this tendency, which is conducive to the maintenance and development of natural group conformity as the basis of the organization's solidarity. It was for this reason that they were ready before World War II to solicit government intervention in order to achieve compulsory membership, at least in such extreme cases as the agricultural associations.

If an organization includes all members in a certain sphere, it is strengthened by the natural feeling of solidarity that already exists among them. In this sense, it may be said that Japanese organizations have the firm support of their members. On the other hand, however, among members of these organizations there is very little sense of commitment to the organization through their own choice. This makes it difficult to mobilize the rank and file for active participation. Although all the members may, on occasion, appear to be taking an active part in something which will enhance group conformity, the activity is not spontaneous. It is rather the result of passive obedience to the leader or to the principle of group conformity. Behind the outward appearance of activity lies a certain apathy.

The Japanese view of organizations as "natural" phenomena is related to another Japanese characteristic—lack of sensitivity to the process of decision-making in the organization. Since many Japanese tend to think that the organization to which they belong exists naturally rather than being something established by them, they tend to feel that the will of the organization will grow naturally out of their conformity. Formal procedures of the organization, such as majority rule and the right of expressing minority opinion, have not been considered very important.

This characteristic may be related, in turn, to the Japanese pattern of communication, in which "silent language" plays an important role.[2] For instance, in Japan the most important qualification for a leader is that he understands what is desired by his followers without explicit discussion. In this sense, the Javanese tradition of *musjawarah*, which means reaching consensus without explicit discussion or at least without voting, has something in common with the Japanese way of decision-making. Very often discontented members form a faction in the hope that it will become so influential that their wishes will be realized, rather than working out their differences with the main group through ordinary organizational procedures. For this reason, the importance of informal leadership, personal relationships, and factional conflict should always be kept in mind in analyzing any Japanese organization.

Batsu

The Japanese term *batsu* is sometimes translated "clique" or "faction," but these English words do not convey the precise meaning of the term. *Batsu* means a private, informal group functioning in the field of public affairs. Such a group is held together by particularly intimate personal ties similar to those in primary groups in rural communities.

This group is characterized by a closed and exclusive unity oriented toward particularistic values, and often involves quasi-familistic relationships—paternalistic protection or patronage on the part of the leader, and dependence on the leader by the rank and file. This quasi-familistic relationship is often called the *oyabun-kobun* relationship (*oya* means parent and *ko* means child). Originally, the *batsu* was based upon traditional solidarity related in some way to the circumstances of birth, but later its basis was broadened to include other than ascriptive qualifications.

The first important *batsu* in modern Japan was the *hanbatsu* (*han* means fief), formed by people from influential fiefs, which played an important role in the Meiji Restoration. Between 1885 and 1918, Japan was led by non-*hanbatsu* prime ministers for only six and a half years. When one prime minister was criticized by a non-*hanbatsu* Diet member, who accused the *hanbatsu* of being despotic, he answered confidently that without the *hanbatsu*, the nation-building would not have been achieved.

After the first imperial and private universities were established and a new method of recruiting competent bureaucrats by special examination was introduced,[3] *gakubatsu* (*gaku* means school) gradually took over the role played by the *hanbatsu*. The *gakubatsu* were formed by the personal ties among those who were graduated from the same university or high school. Family and regional backgrounds were of no importance. At the same time, however, graduation from a particular school, such as Tokyo Imperial University ("Imperial" was dropped from the university's name in 1945) or the First High School, imparted a kind of status not unlike that bestowed by birth.

As the importance of educational background increased, the role played by the *gakubatsu* also became more important. In 1903, 59 percent of the members of the Japanese elite were from ex-samurai families (*shizoku*), who accounted for only 5.6 percent of the total population. In 1911, the proportion was 35 percent, and by 1915 it had fallen to 26 percent. On the other hand, the proportion of members of the elite who had received higher education (university or college) had increased: in 1903 it was 27.5 percent; in 1926, 39 percent; in 1941, 50.3 percent; in 1948, 74.0 percent; and in 1957, 80.5 percent.[4]

Among the elite, the graduates of Tokyo (Imperial) University have occupied many important positions. Particularly noticeable is the percentage of these graduates among bureaucrats: 28 percent in 1903, 47 percent in 1915, 76 percent in 1928, and 35 percent in 1955. Among business leaders, the percentage has been much smaller: 4.6 percent in both 1903 and 1915, 5.7 percent in 1928, and 13.2 percent in 1955.[5] Research conducted in 1962 among 1,500 executives of the 375 highest-ranked companies revealed that 28 percent were graduates of Tokyo University (9 percent were graduates of the Faculty of Law of the university).[6] Because of this sort of privilege, the graduates of Tokyo University have a special sense of solidarity; and in order to compete with them, graduates from other universities also form *gakubatsu*.

The *zaibatsu* (*zai* means finance) or "financial cliques" of prewar Japan are well known. The *zaibatsu* were formed as agents of economic development, with the *zaibatsu* families as their centers. The extended family relationship was the core of the *zaibatsu*, but from the early part of this century, competent men were recruited from outside these families in order that the *zaibatsu* companies might maintain their efficiency. Their number gradually increased, but there were always members of the *zaibatsu* families at the top; and those who joined the *zaibatsu* from outside adopted the pattern of behavior of the *batsu*.

Another *batsu* related to the family system is the *keibatsu* (*kei* literally means sexual relations), which is formed by marriage. The *keibatsu* is often, like adoption, a means of combining the principles of achievement-orientation and familism. For instance, if a family in the elite group finds a competent young man, then it arranges his marriage to a daughter of the family. It often happens that executives of large firms are succeeded by their sons-in-law.

But the *keibatsu* system is not necessarily a means of elevating gifted young men. It may take the form of a dynastic marriage between the offspring of two powerful families. Since marriage in Japan is a link between two families rather than two persons, the personal tie created by marriage becomes the basis for a *keibatsu*. This is one of the reasons why even today family background is considered very seriously at the time of marriage. It is easy to draw family trees of the Japanese elite which are interconnected by marriages with one another. The report that the Crown Prince had become engaged to the daughter of a "commoner" (that is to say, of a man whose family was neither ex-samurai nor ex-nobility) may have created a sensation, but in fact the marriage simply meant that the old class distinctions had been replaced by new ones. There is no doubt that Crown Princess Michiko was born with a silver spoon in her mouth.

One *batsu* that played a very important role in modern Japanese politics was the *gunbatsu* (*gun* means military), or "military clique." It is often said that the *gunbatsu* started the last war. This should not be taken to mean that the military forces, *as an institution*, became so influential that they played the decisive role in national policy-making. The *gunbatsu* was not a formal organization; it was, rather, an informal group that played an important part in decision-making. It is difficult to identify the leader of the *gunbatsu*, but we can at least say that he was not always Minister of the Army, although important positions were often occupied by members of the *gunbatsu*. Advocates of *gunbatsu* policy were to be found among radical young officers. The top leaders in institutional positions were often their puppets. The exercise of influence was also informal, through personal ties. This is one of the reasons why it was so difficult for those who held the top positions to control the *gunbatsu.*

Although the *gunbatsu* and *zaibatsu* were abolished after the war, the *batsu* phenomenon still survives in a different form. The term *habatsu* (*ha* means faction) has a more general meaning than the terms which have been examined so far. *Habatsu* can be seen in almost every organization. Particularly important are those found in political parties. Often *habatsu* are taken to be simply factions within political parties. Studies of party politics in contemporary Japan necessarily deal with *habatsu;* careful examination of party constitutions and other official documents explains less than investigation of the dynamics of the *habatsu.*

The major roles of the leader of a *habatsu* in a political party are: (1) to provide the members of his *habatsu* with money for election campaigns; (2) to give recommendations or other assistance to members of the *habatsu* who wish to become party candidates (this is important because of the lack of primary elections or any other formal procedure to decide party candidates); (3) to help a candidate who is a member of his *habatsu* in an election campaign, for example, by making campaign speeches (this is important because in Japan more than one candidate can be elected from a constituency, and competition is often most fierce between candidates from the same party; (4) to distribute positions such as that of minister and important official posts in the Diet or in the party; (5) to help the members of his *habatsu* to satisfy the demands of their constituents by exerting his influence to provide subsidies for a certain area or group or to pass legislation the members of his *habatsu* have been asked for.

Although each political party in Japan often looks like a coalition of many parties, the *habatsu* cannot be considered a party, because it is formed not on the basis of differences of policy, but on personal ties of patronage and dependence between leader and followers. It also lacks formal procedures, whereas in political parties some sort of formal procedure must exist even if it is only nominal.

Interestingly, the dissolution of the *zaibatsu* was one of the reasons for the emergence of *habatsu* in postwar Japan. Before the war there was a clear link between the two major *zaibatsu* and the two major political parties: the Mitsui *zaibatsu* was associated with the Seiyūkai, and Mitsubishi with the Minseitō. Political funds were secretly given by *zaibatsu* leaders to party leaders. The party leadership was thus all the stronger, since it monopolized the channels through which the party's financial resources flowed. In postwar Japan, however, because of the dissolution of the *zaibatsu*, no adequate single source of funds is available to the political parties. Although an association was organized in business circles to form a pool of political funds to be distributed to the parties, the latter still acquire a considerable part of their funds directly from businesses.

Each *habatsu*, or more precisely the leader of each *habatsu*, collects political funds from individual enterprises and from federations of enterprises. Businessmen are reluctant to give money both to the party as a whole *and* to the individual *habatsu*, but in the present situation they regard it as a necessary evil. Of course, how much is to be given to a particular *habatsu* is determined by the calculations of the businessmen concerning the *habatsu*'s future. An important qualification for the leader of a *habatsu* is therefore the ability to collect funds through personal ties with influential businessmen.

For the rank-and-file Diet member, which *habatsu* to join is a vital question, because it may decide whether or not he is successful in the next election or how soon he gets a ministerial post. But he cannot easily change his *habatsu* even if a group other than the one to which he belongs seems more profitable—first because the *habatsu* is based on personal ties with the leader, and second because if he changes his *habatsu*, his loyalty is suspect, and he is likely to be put at the bottom of the waiting-list for future ministerial posts and may suffer other disadvantages.

Since the *habatsu* is based upon personal ties, a *habatsu* ends once the leader dies. The *habatsu* is either re-formed under a new leader or split into two new *habatsu* led by two former deputy leaders. In fact, it often happens that within a *habatsu* there are many sub-*habatsu* (which are also called *habatsu*). Any unit that has the characteristics described at the beginning of this section may be called a *habatsu*, regardless of size.

Although the manner in which *batsu* appear varies at different times and in different fields, the importance of the *batsu* is more or less constant, in the sense that personal ties which create an informal group cannot be ignored in the analysis of the actual operation of any formal organization. It is worth noting here that the tendency toward more complex and bureaucratized organizations does not result in a diminution in the need for *batsu*; on the contrary, it contributes to their preservation. Therefore, *batsu* should not be viewed as an anachronistic survival, or as an atavistic phenomenon. *Batsu* are a peculiarly Japanese version of the informal groups commonly found in highly developed organizations in contemporary societies.

Political Parties and Interest Groups

Needless to say, political parties are the most important political organizations in any country which has representative government. In Japan, however, political parties are held in very low esteem. It may also be the case in Western countries but more so in Japan. It is not common for ordinary people to join a political party. In the popular mind, political parties are the domain of professional politicians, whose reputation is not always a savory one.

There is a great difference between the number of votes cast for each party and the number of actual party members. The conservative Liberal Democratic party, which has been in power for more than twenty years (with a one-year interruption in 1947 when a coalition cabinet headed by a Socialist prime minister held office), drew 22.3 million votes (47.6 percent of the total) in the general election of 1969, but the party members are mostly limited to those who have obtained public office. Sometimes the number of members is reported by the party (it claimed about 125,000 in 1967), but no one really believes these figures.

The second largest party in terms of votes and of number of seats in the Diet is the Japan Socialist party, which received 10 million votes (21.5 percent of the total) in the 1969 general election. The party claims only about 30,000 members, but the number is not important, because the chief source of support at elections is the General Council of Trade Unions of Japan (Sōhyō), which has a membership of 4 million.

The Democratic Socialist party, which split from the Socialists in 1960, taking a more moderate line on the issue of the security treaty between the United States and Japan, is said to have only 40,000 members, but obtained 3.6 million votes (7.7 percent of the total votes) in the 1969 general election. In this case too, it is supposed that most of the votes were obtained through the labor unions affiliated with the party, which have a membership of approximately a million.

Only the Japan Communist party and the Kōmeitō (Clean Government party, the political arm of the Sōka Gakkai, a Buddhist sect) obtained votes mainly through their party organizations. In the case of the Kōmeitō, votes were obtained, to be more precise, not chiefly through the party, which has 200,000 members, but through the religious organization, which comprises 6 million households. The Kōmeitō succeeded in getting 5.1 million votes (10.9 percent of the total national vote) in the 76 constituencies in which party candidates ran in the 1969 general election. The Communist party, which also has approximately 200,000 members, obtained 3.2 million votes (6.8 percent) with candidates in all 123 constituencies.

The question of how the Liberal Democratic party was able to obtain 22.3 million votes with so few party members will naturally be raised. The Socialist party also received more than 300 times as many votes as it has members, and roughly 2.5 times as many votes as the number of members of its affiliated labor unions. How the rest of the votes were collected is an interesting question.

It is often said that the government party tends to become a party of patronage, whereas the opposition party tends to be a party of principle. This is also true in Japan, probably more so than in many other countries where the ruling party changes more often. Being more or less permanently in power, the Liberal Democratic party has had a monopoly of important public offices, such as ministerial posts, and of the allocation of financial resources, such as government subsidies.

Here mention should be made of the important role played in vote-getting by various interest groups, which are channels for the allocation of financial resources. As has been said, the dependent attitude of organizations toward the government still persists, and because of this attitude, interest groups are willing to provide government party candidates with funds and personnel for conducting election campaigns in order to obtain greater favor with the government. The competition of interest among various organizations accelerates the tendency toward closer relationships between interest groups and influential Diet members and bureaucrats. Of course, under the present circumstances, members of the government party in the Diet are considered to be more influential than those of the opposition party, who can do very little in the process of decision-making concerning the distribution of subsidies or in legislating for special interests.

Relatively powerful interest groups such as those of large industri-

alists have, by means of financial contributions, established close relationships with the party in office, and as a consequence cannot be
ignored by the bureaucrats. These powerful groups do not need to
exert any explicit pressure in order to realize their wishes, although
sometimes corruption is revealed in the matter of financial contributions to the government party: For example, at the time of the passing
of the Government Subsidy and Compensation for Financing the Construction of Ocean Liners Law (1953).[7]

On the other hand, relatively weak organizations such as those of
small and medium-sized enterprises try to balance their requests with
offers of personnel for help in election campaigns, or through their
influence on the votes they control. Although they occasionally exert
organizational pressure on the government party and the bureaucracy
by presenting petitions and holding rallies, their demands are often
whittled down. This is partly due to too great a willingness on their
part to make concessions to the government party, and partly to the
stronger influence of more powerful organizations.

There has been an undeniable tendency on the part of the government party to exploit such interest groups as a substitute for an independent party organization, which is extremely difficult to build in the
present circumstances.

The bureaucracy not only plays an important role both in policy
execution and in policy decision-making, but has also been a partial
substitute for party organization in at least two respects. First, the
bureaucracy has been an important source of supply of competent
candidates for the ruling party, not only because of their knowledge
and experience as bureaucrats, but also because of their influence on
related organizations, such as those that have received subsidies from
the ministry from which the candidate comes.

Second, the bureaucracy can be a link between the government
party, which lacks an independent organization, and the electorate,
which is under the influence of the bureaucracy, because it helps to
determine the distribution of the national budget and of government
subsidies. As long as the conservative party remains in power, its
alliance with the bureaucracy will survive, and so will the relationship
between this complex and the various interest groups.

The policies of a Diet majority based upon this method of collecting
votes may not represent the wishes of a majority of the population. A
gulf can easily open between the policies of the Diet majority and

public opinion, particularly where foreign policy and constitutional issues are concerned, since they can be considered remote from particular group interests.

Because of this gulf, there is room for opposition parties as parties of principle. This is partly the reason why the Socialist parties and the Communist Party have been able to get votes not only through affiliated labor unions, but also from among intellectuals and white collar workers. Particularly when there was a possibility that the conservative party, which has been considering revision of the "Peace" Constitution, would obtain more than two-thirds of the Diet seats, which is a number sufficient to permit the revision of the Constitution, many floating votes were cast for the opposition parties.

Furthermore, if the Diet majority acts with such flagrant disregard for public opinion (as the Kishi cabinet did over the security treaty in 1960, for example) that the majority of people feel it impossible to tolerate its actions, mass protests sometimes take place which serve partly to bridge the gulf between the actions of the Diet majority and public opinion.

Bureaucracy and Judiciary

In contrast to the low esteem in which political parties were held, the social prestige of high-ranking officials in the Japanese bureaucracy (the concept of the "civil servant" did not exist in prewar Japan, so that "bureaucrat" is a more appropriate term) used to be very high. They were considered to be more loyal to the emperor than other sectors of society, particularly businessmen and members of the political parties, who seemed in the popular mind to be pursuing their own group or personal interests. This popular belief in the disinterestedness of bureaucrats meant that their administration was accepted almost without reserve. In the emperor system, which was characterized by a paternalistic relationship between ruler and ruled, the bureaucracy controlled even the details of daily life. For example, during the war, since all personal relationships were subordinated to the "national interest," men and women were forbidden to associate in public. A couple who were seen together, even if they were married, were likely to receive a warning from the police.[8]

The high prestige of the bureaucracy attracted very able recruits.

The special examination introduced in 1887[9] permitted the selection of many of the best candidates. This is one reason why bureaucrats formed the core of the modernizing elite in prewar days. At the beginning of the modern period there was no clear distinction between the higher bureaucrats and the political leaders who were in charge of decision-making. The political leaders in the early Meiji period (roughly the last three decades of the last century) were antipathetic to political parties and were more interested in creating able bureaucrats. Even after the emergence of full-fledged political parties, the first of which was formed by a former Prime Minister, Hirobumi Itō, in 1900, many party leaders were recruited from among high-ranking bureaucrats. In fact, of the more than forty prime ministers of modern history, roughly one-third were recruited from among high-ranking civil bureaucrats.

Imperial prerogatives, since they were actually exercised by the bureaucracy, added to the importance of bureaucrats among the governing elite. After the end of party government in 1932 when Rightist naval officers assassinated the Prime Minister, Tsuyoshi Inukai, who was also the president of the Seiyūkai party, political parties lost their influence, and the role of the bureaucracy became even more important. Later, two other factors further increased the bureaucracy's importance: one was the dissolution of all political parties, which were dissolved into the Imperial Rule Assistance Association in 1940; and the other was the increased role of the bureaucracy in an economy geared to total war. A type of bureaucrat called *shinkanryō* (new bureaucrat) or *kakushin-kanryō* (innovating bureaucrat) emerged among the middle management of the administration. These men were in favor of strengthening government control, and tended to oppose parties and to favor a military regime.

Despite the radical change caused by the defeat and the occupation, even today approximately one-third of the members of the government party in the Diet are ex-bureaucrats. But the social prestige of bureaucrats has declined. Prefectural governors, who were formerly appointed by the Ministry of Home Affairs, are now elected; and Article 68 of the Constitution provides that a majority of cabinet ministers must be members of the Diet. A rise in the social prestige of other occupations, such as business and the professions, has resulted in a decline in the attractiveness of the bureaucracy. Article 41 of the

Constitution states: "The Diet shall be the highest organ of state power"; and the bureaucracy has thus ceased to be the core of the governing elite.

Nevertheless, bureaucrats remain influential, partly because of the weakness of party leadership (which relies heavily on the bureaucracy not only for policy execution, but also in policy formulation and in recruiting able party members), and partly because of the important powers that the bureaucracy still retains (as an agent of the occupation just after the war, and since then as an important institution of the modern planned state). The importance of the bureaucracy, as compared with that of the political parties, is shown by the fact that the number of government bills introduced in the Diet, many of which are initiated by the bureaucracy, is twice as great as that of private members' bills. And the proportion of government bills actually *passed* by the Diet is even higher.[10] Besides the technical skill of bureaucrats in the drafting of legislation, the power of the bureaucracy lies, for example, in the awarding of franchises for new bus services, the ordering and supervision of construction, and so on.

As a result of the postwar reform, bureaucrats are not usually appointed to ministerial positions without first becoming members of the Diet. High-ranking bureaucrats were often appointed to the House of Peers before the war, but this opportunity for promotion has been lost as a result of its abolition. High-ranking bureaucrats who reach a position such as that of vice-minister or bureau chief while still in their forties have to find other jobs outside the bureaucracy; they usually "parachute" into important positions in extragovernmental bodies such as public corporations, or into executive posts in large firms which have close relations with the bureaucracy. Thus, the influence of high-ranking bureaucrats, because of postwar changes, has spread further than even before.

The relations between bureaucracy and business and between bureaucracy and interest groups have become closer than in prewar Japan, because of increased personal ties through "parachuted" personnel. The bureaucracy often helps to weaken the restrictions imposed by the anti-trust laws: evasions of the antimonopoly legislation by business organizations are made possible by skillful drafting and interpretation by bureaucrats, who cover up violations through executive action.

It is usual for bureaucrats to make efforts to obtain as large a share of the budget as possible for those *gaikakudantai* that are related to their ministry or bureau. *Gaikakudantai* (fringe groups) refers to those auxiliary or affiliated groups that are "on the fringe" of the bureaucracy. Their chief functions are to propagate the policies of a particular ministry, sometimes publishing books and magazines for this purpose, and to channel government subsidies into a certain field. Public corporations are often included in this category. Moreover, pressure groups in Japan (for example agricultural cooperatives), which are often interested in obtaining subsidies, tend to become *gaikakudantai* through weakening of their autonomy. *Gaikakudantai* are often criticized on the ground that they are maintained in order to provide posts for retired high-ranking bureaucrats; and in fact, a reduction in their number (there were 303, 63 of them subsidized)[11] was planned in 1955, but nothing came of it. Competition among these groups over allocation of funds has intensified competition among ministries and bureaus and increased sectionalism among bureaucrats, for whom larger subsidies for related organizations mean an increase in their sphere of influence, or at least in their prestige.

The judiciary is, of course, one of the three most important institutions in the modern state. In prewar Japan, judicial decisions were made in the name of the emperor by justices appointed by the emperor (although they were recruited through special examination and could not be dismissed except under extraordinary circumstances). It has often been said that in prewar Japan there was "rule by law" but not "rule of law."[12] Although the imperial will was executed in accordance with the law, it was still confined within the framework of the emperor system, which was above the law. In other words, the law was nothing more than an instrument of imperial rule.

Furthermore, popular feeling was not well disposed toward legal proceedings. Many persons preferred mediation, probably because of the feeling that legal proceedings meant a breakdown in human relations, which many Japanese felt to be supremely important. In fact, the system of mediation in, for example, family disputes and tenant disputes was codified in the 1920s.

After the defeat, the new principle of the "rule of law" replaced the old practice of "rule by law." The independence of the judiciary was, at least formally, guaranteed as strongly as in the West. The social prestige of lawyers, which is an indication of the importance of the judiciary, has improved a great deal. At the end of 1969, 33 (7 percent) out of 486 members of the Lower House of the Diet and 12 (5 percent) out of 250 members of the Upper House were lawyers. This percentage is much the same as before the war—if anything, it is lower and is now decreasing.[13] But this is not because there has been no change in the prestige of lawyers; rather, it is because membership in the Diet is not very attractive to lawyers, who are now both highly respected and very prosperous. It has been reported that some successful lawyers have turned down the opportunity to be recommended by the Bar Association for an appointment to the Supreme Court because it would mean accepting a lower income.

The chief justice of the Supreme Court, who before the war owed his position, in effect, to the Ministry of Justice, is now ranked with the speaker and the prime minister, and has, at least legally, complete independence from the executive and legislative bodies. It should be noted that despite the legally guaranteed independence of the judiciary, the Supreme Court plays a conservative role in Japanese society. This is probably because the justices of the Supreme Court are appointed by the cabinet (nominally by the emperor in the case of the chief justice), which is usually careful to avoid liberal justices, since the government is more or less permanently in the hands of a conservative party.

The conservative character of the Supreme Court can be seen in its decisions, particularly those concerning the Constitution.[14] The Supreme Court justices are usually recruited from among the older judges and lawyers. But compared with older judges who were educated and trained before the war, many younger judges are fairly liberal. There have been some noticeably liberal decisions at the district court level. Among young lawyers, this liberal tendency is much more marked. But it is still too early to assume that this change will eventually reach the highest level of the judiciary, because liberal judges are still "dissenters," and some of them have returned to private legal practice, partly because they cannot expect appropriate promotion and partly because of the attractiveness of the lawyer's position, which is much freer than the judge's, and usually better paid.

Economic Organizations

The organizational structure of the business world was radically changed by the dissolution of the *zaibatsu*. Before the occupation, eleven Mitsui families held 63.8 percent of the total stock of Mitsui companies, and eleven Iwasaki families held 47.8 percent of the stock of Mitsubishi companies. But during the occupation, the *zaibatsu* holding companies, based upon extended family ties, were liquidated, and the individual companies that had been subordinated to them became independent.

It is often said nowadays that there is a tendency toward a revival of the *zaibatsu*. There is indeed a tendency toward oligopoly in leading enterprises, many of which are made up of former *zaibatsu* companies, and toward a closer relationship among those companies that were formerly affiliated with the same *zaibatsu* holding company. Very often the presidents of these companies hold regular meetings. This situation, however, does not indicate a revival of the *zaibatsu*, because the family ties that characterized the *zaibatsu* are no longer important, and the hierarchical structure headed by the holding company and centered around the trading company and the bank has ceased to exist. Instead, the influence of each company within the *zaibatsu* group is determined by its prosperity. Usually the heavy chemical industries occupy the most influential positions.

A similar change has taken place in the internal structure of each company. The necessity for executives to belong to the controlling family, which had already ceased to be an imperative before the war because of the need to increase productivity, became markedly weaker. This was partly because of the purge ordered by the occupation authorities, and partly because it had seemed necessary for executives to keep up with technological innovations. The decline in the importance of owners of capital and the increase in the importance of managers, due to the tendency toward clearer separation between ownership of capital and management, can be seen both in individual enterprises and in the structure of relationships among enterprises in groups composed of former *zaibatsu* companies.

Although the custom of lifetime employment has survived, the seniority rule among employees is not so strong as formerly, and it is now being replaced, at least partly, by the merit system. This is not only the case among white collar workers, but also, perhaps even more so, among blue collar workers, mainly because of rapid technological innovation.

The dissolution of the *zaibatsu* necessitated the formation of new business organizations among the newly independent companies. At first, the formation of a national employers' organization was prohibited by the occupation authorities, who feared the revival of *zaibatsu* influence, and were at that time more interested in encouraging labor unions. Later, however, the Japan Federation of Employers' Associations became so important that it is often jokingly called "the Ministry of Labor in Marunouchi" (Marunouchi is the name of the main Tokyo business district where the federation's office is located).

Another important business organization, the Federation of Economic Organizations (FEO), has been among the most influential interest groups. For example, in 1955 the federation demanded the amalgamation of the conservative parties, which took place soon afterward. The FEO has become the dominant interest group among big business rather than among business as a whole, a fact that reflects the tendency toward oligopoly. This change was illustrated by a reorganization of the FEO in 1952 that excluded small and medium-sized enterprises.[15] In order to compete with the FEO, interest groups also emerged among small and medium-sized enterprises—for example, the Political Federation of Japanese Small Business.

Agricultural interest groups, among which the agricultural cooperatives have been most influential, have also been concerned with defending their own interests, which have been endangered by the tendency toward urbanization. Heavy pressure is brought to bear by the agricultural cooperatives to maintain the producers' price for rice, which is fixed by the government, at an artificially high level. The result is that Japanese rice is more expensive than foreign rice, and so the annual surplus cannot be exported.

Thus, urban Japanese are made to bear a heavier burden in terms of higher cost of living than would be strictly necessary under a different agricultural support policy. On the other hand, the present government policy is one way of reducing the marked income differential between urban and rural workers. Both the government and the agricultural cooperatives realize this fact. The agricultural cooperatives are a channel for the distribution of large amounts of money in the form of government subsidies for rural areas, and hence are in one way heavily dependent on government policy.

Labor unions have been, of course, better able to stand up to business organizations than small business associations or consumer associations. About 36 percent of workers belong to labor unions. Although membership has been increasing in absolute terms, in terms of the percentage of all workers it has remained much the same since 1955.

To foreigners, labor unions may appear to be very radical because of their inclination toward socialism, and appear to be influential because of their strong solidarity.

Their solidarity is buttressed by the ingroup consciousness that comes of their being organized on an enterprise basis, but their influence is also *limited* by the fact that they are enterprise unions in the sense that they cannot afford to be so militant that their actions adversely affect the profits of the enterprise, which is competing with other enterprises in the same field. Particularly in the case of prosperous industries, union members try to increase their wages not so much by obtaining a greater share of the profits, as by increasing the productivity of the enterprise they work for compared with that of competing enterprises. This is part of the reason why many union leaders have a close relationship with the employers and tend not to be very militant in the struggle within the company, although they often pretend to be radical in order to pacify the rank-and-file workers. In addition, it is the more privileged workers who belong to unions, since workers in small and medium-sized enterprises are not as well organized. Therefore it can be said that workers who belong to a union are members of a sort of "establishment" with vested interests.

The influence of labor unions is also restricted by the fact that there is a split between unions affiliated to the Japan Socialist party and those affiliated to the Democratic Socialist party. This split results in conflict within the labor movement. An additional difficulty faced by labor unions is the tendency toward bureaucratization, which often results in the corruption of the leaders in the process of negotiation with the employers. "Corruption" may on occasion mean the actual passing of money, but the word can also be taken to mean that the policies and motives of union leaders have ceased to reflect accurately the desires and hopes of the rank and file of the union. The tendency toward bureaucratization should be examined in the context of contemporary trends to be discussed in Part III.

Part Three
CONTEMPORARY TRENDS

8

The Mass Age

Mass Media

Mass communications media have been developed almost as extensively in Japan as in Western societies. In 1968, the number of newspapers sold per 1,000 persons in Japan was 490, while in the United States the number was 312, and in Britain, 488. In 1966 the number of radio sets per 1,000 persons was 250 in Japan, 1,334 in the United States, and 300 in Britain. In 1968, the number of television sets per 1,000 persons in Japan was 206, while in the United States it was 393, and in Britain, 276. (Since the average number of persons per household is higher in Japan than in the West, the level of penetration of television is higher than would appear from these figures. In 1968, 96 percent of all households in Japan had TV.) If we take into account the fact that the numbers are increasing more rapidly in Japan than in the United States and Britain, we can safely say that there is now virtually no difference in this respect between Japanese and Western societies.

Despite this quantitative similarity, some qualitative differences still exist between the two. One is the fact that the Japanese press is dominated by a few major national papers. National newspapers were already developing rapidly by the late nineteenth century. By the beginning of this century, each of the three largest papers had a circulation of over 100,000. By 1920 the circulation of each of the major national papers had exceeded 1 million. As their circulation grew, their character changed: They turned from papers of opinion into *news*papers. The publishers were so anxious to expand their circulation that they hesitated to express definite political opinions which might have lost them readers. This tendency to avoid adopting a specific political position was also partly the result of the readers' preference for nonpartisan or "neutral" newspapers. In the Japanese political culture, "parties" have been considered to represent "partial" interests and hence have been regarded with suspicion, so that if a newspaper supported a particular party, it ran the risk of being regarded as biased and therefore unreliable. The basis of this way of thinking was the nature of the emperor system, which limited differences of opinion.

Because each of the major national papers tried to appeal to as many people as possible, regardless of their political views, and because of the limitation imposed by the emperor system, the content of all the major papers was very similar. The fierce competition among them was, and continues to be, conducted not so much in terms of content, as by means of various attractions: giving gifts to new subscribers, sponsoring baseball tournaments, holding art exhibitions and concerts. These multiple functions can be seen in other fields of publication, for example, in weekly magazines, and even books. Commercial television channels are not directly owned by newspapers, but have close relationships with them through management and news services.

The existence of three national papers with circulations of over 5 million each means that the majority of the Japanese people see reports on world affairs from the newspapers' foreign correspondents. Some correspondents, such as those in mainland China, in fact, have sent detailed informative reports which no American correspondent could have given, since almost no Americans can enter China. Nowadays, the content of the papers is much more varied than before the war because of the wide range of freedom of expression. Nevertheless, papers other than party organs do not usually express political views, even at election times. The editorials in the major papers are non-committal, and papers do not usually support a particular candidate or take clear sides in disputes over policy.

The same can be said about the content of television. Even the commercial channels have avoided expressing opinions on political matters. The channel operated by NHK (Nihon Hōsō Kyōkai, Japan Broadcasting Corporation), which is a public corporation, is extremely cautious. Since there has been little likelihood of a change of government, NHK has tended to favor the semipermanent government party. Its situation is different from that of the BBC in Britain where the possibility, or probability, of a change of government has ensured the maintenance of its neutrality.

The importance of the role played by television has increased rapidly. According to research conducted in 1960,[1] Japanese over the age of ten, including those who did not have a set at home, watched television for an average of 56 minutes every weekday. Between 1960 and 1964, the average time spent watching television increased three times. This can easily be accounted for by the rapid increase in the number of television sets. Already in 1960 the average time spent watching television by those who had sets at home was 2 hours and 20 minutes a day. The increase in the amount of leisure time spent watching television has resulted in a decrease in the time spent in reading[2] and in going to theaters and concerts. The number of cinemas reached a peak of 7,457 in 1960, and has since been declining. By 1960 the average time spent reading newspapers and magazines on a weekday had fallen to 29 minutes.

The change in the use of leisure time caused by the increased influence of television is not simply a question of the amount of time spent in front of the set: it also includes a change in attitudes. As is the case in many countries, the overwhelming influence of television creates a stereotyped response in the audience and thus contributes to conformity in popular attitudes. This is especially the situation in Japan, where there has been a long tradition of national homogeneity and conformity. There is an anecdote about a mother infected with "education fever" who urges her child to study hard instead of watching television, but tells him that she will watch a popular program for him and let him know the story later, so that he will not be left out of his friends' discussion of it.

The strength of the influence of television may be illustrated by the results of the election for the Upper House in June 1968. Several television stars who ran in the election scored surprising successes: One television actor received 1.2 million votes; a comedian, 0.7 million; a television commentator and novelist, 1 million; and a young novelist whose brother is a popular actor in films and television, 3 million. (The last two were candidates of the government party, and the first two were independent.) Some newspaper commentators said that the influence of television had overcome the influence of organizations. And it is a fact that many candidates supported by labor unions and other national organizations were unsuccessful, whereas in previous elections, candidates, particularly for the national constituency, were elected mostly through the support of nationwide organizations.

Television has a stronger and more direct impact on its audience than any other medium of communication. Live broadcasts can make the audience feel that they themselves are present. This reaction could be seen when the nuclear-powered aircraft carrier *Enterprise* visited Sasebo in western Japan, and caused fierce protest; and again when an American jet fighter crashed on the campus of the University of Kyūshū, evoking a strong protest from the people in the area. These incidents were televised and made such a strong impression on the audience that they immediately became national issues inviting nationwide responses.

However, as elsewhere, attention is fragmented by television, which shows widely different scenes in rapid succession: a few minutes' news about the talks between America and North Vietnam in Paris may be followed by a beauty contest. This fragmentation counterbalances the effect of the vivid presentation of information, and so television may encourage rather than dispel the political apathy of mass society.

Some of the responses evoked by television news coverage are expressed by means of letters to the editors of various newspapers. The increase in the number of letters to the editor is one of the most notable changes in popular attitudes toward newspapers. For instance, in June 1960 when the security treaty between the United States and Japan was revised and the planned visit of President Eisenhower was canceled because of the resulting disturbances, three times as many letters as in a normal month were sent to the editors of the three major national papers (6,938 to *Asahi*, 4,683 to *Mainichi*, and 3,390 to *Yomiuri*); and the majority of them were serious discussions of the treaty issue and of the conduct of the Administration. The next peak in the number of letters came in 1965, the year the United States started bombing North Vietnam: sixty thousand letters were sent to the editor of *Mainichi* within the year. In January 1968, the month the *Enterprise* visited Sasebo, 8,163 letters were sent to the editor of *Asahi*, of which 2,516 were directly concerned with the *Enterprise* issue. When a series of ten articles written by a correspondent in Vietnam appeared in *Asahi* in 1967, 3,390 letters were sent to the editor expressing readers' views on the articles. And the response to an appeal in one letter for

English translations of the articles to be sent abroad, particularly to America, resulted in the dispatching of thirty thousand copies within a year.

Besides the increase in the number of letters, it is an important fact that these letters are widely read. Research conducted by the Japan Newspaper Publishers and Editors Association in 1967 shows that 37.4 percent of the people interviewed read the letters to the editor, a higher percentage than read the editorials (28.8 percent). Furthermore, the proportion of those who read the letters to the editor rose 7 percent between 1961 and 1967.[3] This is one indication that more people than before are responding positively to newspapers. Particularly noticeable is the increase in popular sensitivity to political issues related to the problem of war and peace. The number of those who send letters to the editor, a few thousand a month, is still relatively small compared with a circulation of several million (5.35 million in 1967 in the case of *Asahi*), but it is worth mentioning this increasingly positive response.

Mass Consumption and Leisure

The rapid increase in mass consumption and leisure is a phenomenon common to all highly industrialized societies. Japan's annual 9 percent growth in consumption in the period 1960–1965 was the fastest in the world. Particularly noteworthy in this period was the rapid distribution of durable consumer goods. The rate of diffusion of refrigerators among households stood at 77.6 percent in 1968, and that of washing machines at 84.8 percent.

This widespread distribution of durable consumer goods has increased leisure time. The average daily leisure time in 1941 was 4.3 hours among white collar workers and 3.3 hours among blue collar workers, while the average in 1960 was 5.2 hours.[4] This increase occurs in any highly industrialized society. How people *use* their leisure time, however, differs from country to country. Let me illustrate some of the differences.

One characteristic feature of Japan is that use of leisure time differs comparatively little among classes. There is a clear contrast here with Britain, for example. Research conducted by the BBC in 1961 showed that the percentages of those watching television at 8 P.M. were 30 percent among the upper middle class, 35 percent among the lower middle class, and over 40 percent among the lower class, while in Japan the percentage in 1965 was between 45 and 50 percent regardless of differences of class and income.[5]

This sort of homogeneity may be seen in the United States, too, but there is an important difference between the United States and Japan in that in Japan a striking contrast may be seen between different generations. Rather than differences in income, occupation, and educational background, in Japan differences of generation is the most important of the variables that correlate with differences in use of leisure time. For instance, mountainclimbing, hiking, baseball and other energetic pastimes are popular among young Japanese, while the older generations are fond of gardening, *go*, golf and other quieter pursuits. This difference is not attributable solely to the physical superiority of youth over age; it is partly due to the belief that particular kinds of behavior are appropriate to particular times of life. The contrast is much clearer in Japan than in the United States, and is but one of many indications of the great gulf between generations in Japan.

Another characteristic is that leisure is often spent in group activities. For instance, among a sample interviewed in Tokyo in 1965, 76 percent had spent one or more nights away from home within the previous year, half of them as members of groups.[6] It is very common in Japan for a group of employees (and their bosses) to go on tours either sponsored or subsidized by their company. Leisure is the time at one's own disposal, but in Japan it may be spent in company activities that are felt to be necessary in order to maintain harmonious personal relationships. Recently, family trips and tours by spontaneous groups (which are often composed of peer members of the same company) have become more common, but even trips of this sort are not completely independent of the company, since they often make use of company lodges and other facilities.

A third characteristic is the high degree of "inter-consumer demonstration effect." This may be illustrated by the very high expenditure on entertainment shown in Figure 2. Such expenditure probably indicates that many people spend more money than they can afford in order to demonstrate their prosperity. If we consider this "status-spending" together with the relatively low level of expenditure on food (less than 40 percent of total income) compared with the low level of per capita income in Japan, we may deduce that many people skimp expenditure on food in order to spend the money on leisure

Figure 2. Expenditure on Entertainment

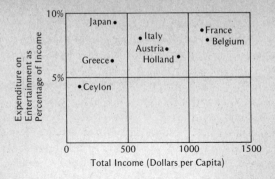

SOURCE: *Kokuminseikatsu Hakusho (White Paper on Standards of Living)*, 1964, p. 241.

activities. It often happens, in fact, that a housewife has to go without meat in order to buy a *kimono*, which may cost more than her husband earns in a month, because at PTA meetings or friends' weddings she will feel uncomfortable if she is not as well dressed as the other women present. Her husband may spend a great deal of money on drinking with his fellow workers or customers in order to maintain good personal relationships with them (although in the latter case the expenses are often paid by the company); or he may buy ski clothes in order to go on skiing trips with his fellow workers. Thus, traditional Japanese group conformity has intensified the orientation toward consumption that is found in many developed societies.

Frugality, which was considered a great virtue in prewar Japan, partly because of Confucian influence and partly because of the traditional samurai ethic, is not in evidence among young people today. Instead, most of them have adopted a new slogan, "consumption is a virtue." For instance, as early as 1961, research conducted in Tokyo showed that 47.7 percent of those interviewed who were between the ages of 20 and 24 agreed with this slogan, while only 20.8 percent of those who were between 55 and 59 agreed with it.[7] Here again, we see a great difference between generations. Ironically enough, the fact that frugality is no longer esteemed has meant that expenditure on entertainment and leisure activities has been increased by the consumer's desire to demonstrate his prosperity, so that he may, as a result, exercise an enforced frugality in matters not observed by others, such as expenditure on food.

Of course, the high degree of consumption orientation is partly the result of the influence of advertising, as in many other developed societies. Advertising expenditure, which has already reached 2 percent of the national income, is increasing rapidly. National income tripled in the ten years from 1952 to 1962, while expenditure on advertising multiplied 6.3 times.[8] Needless to say, the role of the mass media in carrying advertisements is very important. Leveling of consumption resulting from the postwar reforms, such as dissolution of the *zaibatsu*, land reform, and the encouragement of the labor movement, has prepared the ground so that people respond to advertisements in almost the same way regardless of occupation and income. The increase in the number of those who think that they belong to the middle class (87 percent in 1964, a 6 percent increase within six years),[9] also encourages the leveling of taste in consumption.

A good example of the creation of mass consumption by commercialism in general and by advertising in particular is the Japanese attitude toward Christmas. In 1964, half of a group interviewed by *Yomiuri* said that they sent gifts, had a special dinner, and so on at Christmas, whereas only 1 percent said that they were Christians.[10] For the majority of the Japanese, Christmas is not a time for religious celebration, but for Christmas sales in the department stores. St. Valentine's Day was not known by most Japanese until very recently, but chocolate manufacturers are now popularizing it in order to sell more of their products.

Mass Culture

The leveling of taste is also occurring in the case of cultural products. As early as 1925, as many as 740,000 copies of the first issue of a popular monthly magazine called *King* were sold. Its circulation expanded so rapidly that it had reached 1.4 million by 1933. Its publisher, Kōdansha, was jokingly called "the private ministry of education."

In the same period another company, Iwanami, published a large number of books on philosophy and the social sciences widely read among intellectuals, whose number, of course, was at that time still limited. *Sōgōzasshi* (cultural reviews), periodicals containing articles and essays of high quality on philosophy and the social sciences, social and political criticism, and fiction were also widely read in this circle.

In postwar Japan, however, the distinction between the readers of popular magazines and the readers of "cultural" periodicals has become much less clear than before, because of the development of higher education. Nowadays, people in universities and colleges account for 20 percent of their age group in the population as a whole. This figure is the same as the percentage of people in middle schools one generation before. But this rise in level of education does not necessarily mean that the quality of widely read books has risen. In fact, serious periodicals are outnumbered by popular magazines, and much of the influence of serious books is replaced by that of debased "popular" books. This may easily be confirmed by examining the list of best-selling books in the postwar period. The large number of paperback books of popular fiction is another indication of this tendency.

It is probably an oversimplification, however, to say that Japanese cultural activities have been degenerating in the mass society, although it is partly true. Today, a much larger number of people than ever before are exposed to a wide range of ideas, from those of Sartre and Nkrumah to those of Malcolm X. The high proportion of translations among the total of books published reveals one important characteristic of Japanese culture. In 1966, 30,451 books were published, of which 1,227 were translations (707 from English, 171 from French, 145 from German, 117 from Russian; 447 in the social sciences, 267 in natural science, and 481 in the arts). The list of best-selling books in postwar Japan includes such items as translations of *War and Peace* (chiefly because of the popularity of the movie of the same title) and of Simone de Beauvoir's *The Second Sex*.

It is surprising how rapidly books are translated into Japanese. For instance, two different Japanese translations of Che Guevara's *Bolivian Diary* were published within a few months of the appearance of the original in Havana; and the Japanese version of *The Trumpet of Conscience* by Martin Luther King also came out within a few months of the original publication. The cultural variety of books translated is also impressive: they range from Chinese to American, from philosophy to fashion. Before the war, intellectuals were strongly attracted to European culture, but nowadays tastes have broadened, and there is a much greater variety of books.

How is a wide variety of cultural products able to exist in the same society, and what are the relationships among them? Karl Loewith, who taught German philosophy in Japan between 1936 and 1941, wrote in the introduction to the Japanese translation of his book *Nihilismus in Europa* that Japanese society could be explained by the metaphor of a two-story house: on the second floor was a throng of philosophers from Plato to Heidegger, while on the first floor the Japanese people followed their traditional ways of thought and behavior. Loewith wondered where the stairway was that connected the two floors. This metaphor neatly explains the cultural situation in prewar Japan, but in the postwar period, there has been only one floor, on which every cultural product is displayed as in a supermarket.

The same person does not usually buy many different kinds of books: He may be particularly interested in Chinese Communist publications, or in popular American fiction, or in French books on fashion. In the same way, hundreds of thousands of people visit the United States and more than a thousand visit mainland China every year, but very few have visited both. Particular groups are often marked by attachment to a particular culture or country: An enthusiasm for French culture *as a whole* is common among people working in fashion, a field in which France has been traditionally preeminent, and an enthusiasm for German culture *as a whole* or American culture *as a whole* is common among sociologists, depending on which country has had the greater influence on their thought. There is very little communication between people who belong to different groups. The various cultures exist in compartments like those of a railway train, with access to a common corridor, but with no connecting doors.

It may happen that one sometimes conforms to the mood of one group and sometimes to that of another group, even if the two attitudes are inconsistent. Most Japanese are married in a Shintō ceremony and buried with Buddhist rites. Shintō and Buddhist practices coexist without being synthesized, and they are not understood to be alternatives.

The existence of a colorful variety of different cultural elements, preserved separately in distinct groups, is not a source of creativity because of the lack of contact between them. Each group retains a stereotyped image of a particular culture that is influenced very little by elements from other cultures.

No doubt passive acceptance of stereotyped images perpetuated by the mass media is found in any mass society, but in Japan different stereotyped images exist in different groups. It is a paradoxical contrast between the American and the Japanese cultural situations that although in the latter more national homogeneity is seen than in the former, nevertheless a wider variety of opinions and images can be found. It may be said that in Japan the habit of group adoption of elements from foreign cultures represents in itself a sort of cultural homogeneity. Even the behavior of dissenters in the United States, such as the hippies, has become a fashion in one closed group in Japan. Interestingly, dissenters form groups with "conformity of alienation."[11]

This tendency to introduce foreign patterns of behavior and cultural elements as a group has persisted for a long time. Only recently has it begun to change. This change has two causes, one external—pluralization of cultural models; the other internal—difficulty in group conformity. The Sino-Soviet split and recent Russian oppression in Czechoslovakia on the one hand, and the civil rights, peace, and student movements in the United States on the other hand, have brought home to many Japanese the fact that it is difficult to find an ideal, unchanging model abroad. However, this change is merely an external one, and it is still possible to look for a new model: Che Guevara's philosophy, or the theories of Herbert Marcuse, or whatever it may be.

The second of these changes, an internal one, however, has had a deeper influence than the first. As the sense of alienation in mass society grows, distrust in group conformity has emerged because of the stagnation that results from it. Dependence on the group is so strong that disillusionment with the group is a serious matter. A sort of anarchistic attitude, or at least its embryo, can be seen particularly among young people. What the result of this new tendency will be is still uncertain. At the moment, however, its importance should not be exaggerated; although it may be influential as a destructive factor—for example, in one small sector of the student movement—it will not be capable in the immediate future of achieving much positive effect, so long as the sole motivation is destructive without any constructive element. This emergence of anarchistic attitudes, together with another recent tendency, the emergence of civic attitudes, will be discussed in more detail when we deal with the problem of bureaucratization and alienation.

9

Rapid Social Change

Urbanization

The clearest indication of rapid urbanization in Japan is the extraordinary change in the distribution of population. In 1930 the percentage of those engaged in primary industry was 49.3; by 1965 it had fallen to 24.7, and it is still decreasing. The change shows, of course, that many people from rural areas have moved to urban areas to engage in secondary and tertiary industries. This rural exodus has caused overcrowding in urban areas (the difficulties produced by this situation were described in Chapter 6).

Another result is a shortage of labor in general, and of young people in particular, in rural areas. When a field survey was conducted in a village near a city in western Japan in 1961, twenty-six mothers of the thirty interviewed said that they wanted their sons to be white collar workers. Only two wanted their sons to follow in their fathers' footsteps on the land.

A national survey in 1960 showed that only 4.7 percent of those who graduated from middle school in that year and 4.5 percent of those who graduated from high school went into agriculture. It is often said that those young men who have decided to stay in their villages have difficulty finding suitable wives because of the unpopularity of farm life among girls. This is, of course, largely due to the lag in income and standards of living between urban and rural areas, although life in rural areas has improved since the war. Eighty percent of farming families also engage in some business other than agriculture in order to supplement their income.

For farmers, psychological discontent and anxiety are now more serious than the poverty of their physical environment. Because of the leveling of desires and the influence of the mass media, their expectations of improvement in the quality of their lives are rising much faster than the actual improvement; and there is a conspicuous difference in standards of living between urban and rural areas. Thus, discontent among farmers has been aggravated.

Furthermore, many can see no hope for the future; on the contrary, they feel that farming is a declining industry. This view is partly correct. Agriculture in Japan has long been supported financially by the government because of the need for self-sufficiency during the last war and for political stabilization after it. Now, however, the government would like to put an end to this financial support, which has become a heavy burden. Since farmers have long been accustomed to depend on the government, their fear of being abandoned has created a deep and widespread anxiety. This anxiety is undoubtedly among the most important of the reasons why so many village mothers want their sons to be white collar workers. A large number of young people have, in fact, left their villages, although the situation they have found in the cities is not much better unless they have had good educational backgrounds.

Even those whose families left their villages a generation or more ago, and who have been city dwellers all their lives, are not always as content as farmers imagine. Besides the difficulties resulting from urban problems, they lack the warm personal ties that exist between relatives and neighbors in the same village. In every society, urbanization means that the individual is emancipated from the communal life of the rural community, and in this sense has more freedom than before; but at the same time, it means that he becomes "a crab without its shell,"[1] with less protection by the primary groups to which he belongs, and a greater sense of isolation and helplessness.

Although this double-edged effect can be seen in the process of urbanization everywhere, personal difficulties are particularly serious when urbanization takes place so quickly that people are unable to prepare psychologically to face the new situation. Furthermore, urbanization in Japan was largely a result of rapid and artificially induced

industrialization, and hence various conflicts arose from unbalanced
development: for example, strong resentment among the farming
population against industrialization and urbanization; or nostalgia for
communal life among city dwellers who still had contact with their
home villages, and who had always at the back of their minds the
knowledge that they could return if the lack of social security in the
cities made it necessary—if they fell ill, or when they retired. This
situation was utilized by the militarist regime, which turned resentment aganst urbanization into resentment against Westernization,
since the two were often identified.[2]

The situation in Japan today has changed in the sense that those who
have uprooted themselves from their home villages do not have a firm
enough social basis there to feel nostalgia for the communal "good old
days." But so long as the uneven development continues, there will
always be problems due to the imbalance between the urban and rural
sectors. An agricultural support policy that maintains the price of rice
at an artificially high level inevitably leads either to a heavy financial
burden on the government or to a high cost of living for consumers,
for whom rice is still the principal food.

The government's agricultural support policy, aimed chiefly at the
maintenance of political stability within the farming community,
which formerly constituted a majority of the population, is now being
reconsidered, because of the financial burden and because of the increasing demand among consumers for an end to further rises in food
prices. Although the farming segment is now less than one-fourth of
the total population, the government cannot ignore the political importance of rural areas, for they form the base of the government
party's support, and they are electorally overrepresented because of
the lack of reapportionment. But the trend toward urbanization,
which has been changing Japanese society rapidly, is ineluctable.
Sooner or later the government will have to confront the necessity of
taking some positive action in response to this rapid change.

The problem of urbanization is not limited to the conflict between
the rural and urban sectors. The tendency toward an increased sense
of isolation and helplessness is a serious problem among city dwellers.
So far, many workers who belong to large enterprises have been able
to depend on established organizations such as their company or its
labor union. As the organizations grow and become huge bureaucratized bodies, however, the sense of alienation makes the "crab

without its shell" feel completely helpless. This tendency is intensified by technological innovation, which depersonalizes the process of production.

Technological Innovation

Technological innovation is a phenomenon common to all highly industrialized societies, but its causes and consequences are not always the same. Some causes of technological innovation peculiar to Japan are present in her internal situation and international circumstances.

Lack of natural resources makes it necessary for Japan to import such basic raw materials as iron and oil. Of course, the cost of raw materials is therefore higher than in most other industrial societies, and this handicap has to be compensated for. Before the war, cheap labor served this purpose, but since the war, with the development of the union movement, wages have risen, so that in order to overcome this handicap now, it is necessary to improve technology so as to produce goods more efficiently and cheaply than competing countries. Moreover, recent rapid economic growth has caused a shortage of manual workers (particularly young manual workers), which has resulted in further wage increases. Thus, dependence on sophisticated machines rather than on sheer manpower has increased.

Another factor that encourages technological innovation is international competition strengthened by the liberalization of foreign trade which began in the early 1960s. In July 1967, Japan also took the first important step toward the liberalization of capital transactions. The Japanese economy has now to face fierce international rivalry in which technological competition plays an important part.

According to research carried out in a steel works, production increased by 57.2 percent between 1951 and 1957, while the number of workers decreased by 9.7 percent. In many factories production per worker doubled during this period.[3] The steel industry as a whole developed so rapidly that, for instance, between 1951 and 1960 production of hot-rolled stainless steel increased 27.5 times, from 6,427 tons in 1951 to 176,752 tons in 1960, making Japan the world's third largest manufacturer of stainless steel. Technological innovation has also brought about great changes in transportation and communication. The super-express trains of the New Tōkaidō Line connect Tokyo and Osaka (345 miles) in about three hours, and the Post

Office now uses automatic letter-sorting machines which "read" a postal code.

Rather than multiplying the many examples of this sort, it will be useful to examine the consequences of technological innovation in Japan. One characteristic feature shown by several studies is a less favorable popular attitude toward technology than in other developed countries. A nationwide public opinion poll conducted by the *Yomiuri* in 1968[4] reveals that only 37.5 percent of interviewees approved of the effect on their lives of the introduction of computers ("makes life more convenient," 21.2 percent; "makes work easier," 13.1 perecent; and so on); while more than half of the respondents disapproved ("causes sackings," 12 percent; "causes further depersonalization," 38.2 percent).

This negative attitude of the Japanese toward technological innovation should not be interpreted simply as conservatism or explained merely in psychological terms, since the introduction of new machines sometimes does in fact increase the worker's burden. A study carried out in an iron foundry, for example, showed that while only 14 percent of workers said they were less tired after the introduction of a new machine, 48 percent said they were more tired.[5]

Technological innovation is modernizing the process of production and reducing the importance of the acquisition of skills that require long training. Thus the traditional seniority rule, which has favored long-trained workers, is now being threatened. Sooner or later, it will be replaced by a merit system. This change has indeed already begun, but for the time being conflicts between seniority and merit will continue. In order to avoid these conflicts, some employers make special arrangements when they introduce new machines: they may even establish a new company with new workers, thereby avoiding labor union protests.

Technological innovation has also brought about changes in management. It demands a great deal of capital investment, and thus necessitates enlargement of the scale of enterprise. The result has been an increase in corporate mergers. The number of mergers in Japan averaged 400 a year in the latter half of the 1950s, but began to increase sharply in the mid-1960s. In 1967, it soared to 995. A recent example is the merger between the Yawata and Fuji Iron and Steel companies, which has formed the second largest iron and steel company in the world. The dual structure of the Japanese economy includes not only the huge corporations created by these mergers, but also many small and medium-sized enterprises. The increase in size of highly developed enterprises widens the gulf between them and the smaller ones, whose consequent lack of bargaining power puts them in a weaker position vis-à-vis the huge companies from which they obtain much of their work through subcontracts. Increases in their share of the market by these huge enterprises may endanger the interests of consumers, who are unrepresented by a well-organized interest group. And within the huge enterprises, bureaucratization leads to an increased sense of alienation among employees.

Bureaucratization and Alienation

The recent phenomenon of oligopoly composed of huge bureaucratized organizations is a characteristic consequence of "the age of organization."[6] ("Oligopoly" conventionally refers to the concentration of *economic* power in a small number of very large-scale concerns. Here, however, its meaning is not restricted to the field of economics.) In Japan, just as in many other developed societies, a phenomenon which may be called "the eruption of groups"[7] is observable. Immediately after the end of the occupation, this phenomenon developed so rapidly and widely that it attracted great popular attention. The emergence of interest groups, or pressure groups, was one instance. Besides the general circumstances—such as differentiation of interests—that give rise to this phenomenon in any developed society, two other factors were directly connected with its appearance in Japan. In different ways, both arose from the ending of the occupation. First, there was no longer any superior body such as that which had in the initial stages of the occupation prevented the formation of a national federation of employers' organizations and the concentration of economic power. Second, because the process of decision-making now became independent of external influences, interest groups began to play a more important role.

The increased importance of various groups and organizations attracted so much popular attention that the individual's significance in this development was not clearly recognized. The underestimation of the role of the individual was also due to the traditional Japanese view of organizations as organic entities. The long tradition of group conformity encouraged the "eruption of groups," and intensified the competition among various groups. Fierce competition resulted in the late 1950s in the oligopoly of a small number of huge organizations. Oligopolies exist in both the political and the economic arenas: in the former, as a clear distinction between the "ins" led by the semipermanent government party and the "outs" led by the opposition parties; in the latter, as the concentration of economic power in a few huge corporations.

Each organization in this oligopoly has become vast in size and bureaucratized in its organizational structure. The tendency toward bureaucratization of these huge organizations has been encouraged by the traditional Japanese view of an organization as a natural phenomenon—a view which ignores the importance of the process of decision-making. If an organization is based upon natural group conformity and at the same time the traditional view of it as an organic entity persists, there appears what may be called "*carte blanche*" leadership,[8] that is, leadership based on the unconditional and unanimous dependence of the rank and file on their leader without specification of their demands, but with the general expectation that services will be rendered to them by the leader.

An impersonal bureaucratic structure is always accompanied by difficulties, but in Japan, because of the general apathy of the members of organization toward the process of decision-making and because of the *carte blanche* leadership structure, there are few avenues for ameliorating them. The outcome is a restless discontent among the rank and file that cannot be resolved satisfactorily by existing procedures. The increased discontent felt both by the rank and file within the organizations and by the people outside them has resulted in a growing sense of alienation. This sense of alienation, which often takes the form of distrust of and resentment against huge organizations, either makes people lapse into a state of resignation or creates "indignants." Both types are included in the category of political apathy by David Riesman and Nathan Glazer.[9]

It must not be thought, however, that the tendencies toward increased bureaucratization and an increased sense of alienation are proceeding hand-in-hand without hindrance. Recently, in the late 1960s in particular, distrust has been directed not simply toward the government party and other organizations that compose the established politico-economic order, but also toward the existing opposition parties and associated organizations such as the labor unions. In fact, the labor unions, which have now joined the ranks of huge established organizations with bureaucratic structures, have tended to be concerned with their vested interests, or more specifically with those of their leaders. Thus, the people's sense of alienation has become stronger than ever before. It is ironic that the age of organization should have brought about in many people's minds a tendency toward de-organization, that is the increased distrust in established organizations.

Increased political apathy is not the only possible result of this tendency; it may lead to the emergence of the consciousness of individuality. Although still few in number, some discontented people are beginning to realize they have only themselves to depend on and to feel they ought to take action on their own initiative. Sometimes they are so distrustful of the leadership of huge organizations that they form very small groups for various civic movements which can easily be controlled by the members themselves. In fact, Japan now has for the first time a multitude of voluntary groups ("voluntary" in a strict sense) that tackle urban problems, for instance, or campaign for peace, particularly for the removal of American military bases.

The tendency toward de-organization is purely negative in the sense that it simply represents emotional antipathy against organizations, and we cannot look forward to the spontaneous growth of individualism from this tendency alone. Dependence on the group is not weak enough to disappear simply because of this negative element. However, if we also consider the fact that the principles of the Constitution have gradually taken root in the popular mind, the recent appearance of a number of civic groups may be viewed as an indication of a new tendency which may be called the "emergence of citizenship."[10] But it is still too early to conclude from the limited emergence of civic movements that there has been a full emergence of civic consciousness, which Japan has long lacked. The opposite tendency toward the "eclipse of citizenship,"[11] which results from characteristics common to mass society, such as bureaucratization, is also seen in Japan. The question of whether citizenship will develop or be eclipsed must be examined in the broader context of popular attitudes.

10

Popular Attitudes and Opinions

Major Popular Concerns

According to various public opinion polls, the answer most frequently given to the question "What is your chief concern in life?" is "my family." For instance, in a poll conducted by *Yomiuri* in 1968 using a national sample of 10,000 persons between 15 and 79 years of age, 24.1 percent answered "my family," and 24.4 percent, "my children."[1] To the question "What is the greatest hindrance to a contented life?" the most frequent answer was "high prices" (30.3 percent). In a poll conducted by NHK (Japan Broadcasting Corporation) in the same year, in answer to the question "What are you most concerned about?" high prices was ranked first (78.1 perecent) and the war in Vietnam second (51.7 percent—interviewees could mention more than one issue).

If high prices is the most important popular concern, what do people think is the cause for them? The *Yomiuri* poll shows that 28 percent of the interviewees mentioned the government's poor economic policy (25.9 percent referred to the increase in the price of rice, which is related to economic policy). Salaries and wages have not always kept up with the rapid rise in consumer prices. Consumer prices in Tokyo in September 1968 were 7.4 percent higher than in September 1967; and the number of those who felt that they were better off (14 percent) was much lower than that of those who felt they were worse off (32 percent).[2] It is easy to see that there is a wide gulf between the increased desire for consumption and the ability to satisfy it, since the rise in incomes must not merely match but actually exceed the rise in prices in order to meet higher expectations. When the respondents to the *Yomiuri* poll were asked whether they believe that Article 25 of the Constitution, which states "all people shall have the right to maintain the minimum standards of wholesome and cultured living," is observed, 36.6 percent answered negatively ("this right is not protected," 25.8 percent, "this article simply states an ideal," 10.8 percent).

If the majority of the people are concerned over high prices and many consider the chief cause to be the government's poor economic policy, how do they think that policy can be changed? Curiously enough, despite their awareness of the effect of economic policy on daily life, few people take these policies into account when casting their votes. A survey of candidate choice in November 1963 reveals that only 5.6 percent voted for particular policies, and only 23.2 percent for a particular party, while 54.4 percent voted for "the candidate."[3] That is to say, voters were concerned less with the policies a candidate advocated or the party he belonged to than with his personal relationship with the voters and his personal influence in the political arena. The importance of this sort of "standing" (*jinbutsu*) is not merely "conservatism." The voters do not necessarily respect the candidate simply because of his status. Rather, they vote for a candidate who has the influence necessary to get things done for them, and from whom they can expect some return. In this sense, the voters are trying in a practical way to obtain a larger share of the budget for their district or for the group to which they belong, since the candidate with greater political influence can more easily satisfy this expectation.

From the candidate's point of view, the crucial problem is how to stimulate and also to satisfy expectations of this sort. Immediately after the general election of 1967, each successful candidate was interviewed and asked what, in his view, was the most important factor in his success. The most frequent answer was "my supporters' club" (28.2 percent); next was "my appeal to local interests" (15.2 percent).[4] The "supporters' club" is chiefly composed of representatives of groups that expect their demands to be realized by the candidate. The candidate cannot depend merely on his ascriptive status or prestige (although it is indeed an additional advantage); he must exert himself to prove he will be useful to the voters. One successful candidate declared with pride that the secret of his success was the three-foot-high pile of letters he had written within the previous year on behalf of people in his constituency (recommendations for jobs, interventions with officials of private universities to secure places for students with insufficiently high grades, letters to the police to persuade them not to prosecute for minor offenses).[5] The majority of voters know which candidate will be most useful to them in the short run, but are not sophisticated enough to realize which policy will be most valuable to them in the long run.

A similar limitation in the range of popular interest is seen in concern with the organization. Because of the traditional strength of identification with the organization, the importance of the organization in the mind of the individual is sometimes almost as great as that of the family. A national opinion poll conducted by *Mainichi* in 1968 posed a hypothetical question: "Suppose Mr. A had arranged to go on a trip with his family, but later it turned out that an outing of his co-workers had been organized for the same day. If you were Mr. A, what would you do?" Forty-five percent answered that they would go on the trip with their families, and 44 percent that they would go with their colleagues.[6]

If popular concern is mostly limited to the immediate situation, whether it is family or other group, how is it that the second most important issue in the popular mind is the war in Vietnam? This seeming contradiction can probably be explained by the fact that the Japanese people do not feel the war is remote from their daily lives: first, they are extremely sensitive about war because of their experience of bombing—particularly the atomic bombings, 313,161 of whose victims still survived in 1967;[7] second, the war in Vietnam means for many Japanese an increase in the difficulties caused by American military bases, such as airplane crashes, GI misconduct, and prostitution. In these two senses the war, even though it is being fought in Vietnam, is felt by many Japanese to affect their daily lives. So long as this sort of feeling continues, the issue will occupy an important position in the popular mind, despite the powerful popular interest in immediate life circumstances.

This situation is similar to that concerning civil liberties, in the sense that not many people are particularly interested in fundamental human rights as a principle, but when a threat to civil liberties, such as the planned amendment of the Police Duties Execution Law in 1958, is felt to affect daily life, it becomes a source of deep concern. The planned amendment attempted to strengthen police authority, but this attempt reminded older people of their experience in the police state during the war and made younger people feel that their privacy would be threatened by the police. The title of an article in a popular weekly magazine, "Police Law Will Imperil Dating," epitomized the widespread popular concern with this issue. In the same way, when people felt that the "peace" Constitution was endangered by the government's avowed intention to revise it, the opposition party used with great effect the slogan, "Boys! Don't take up arms! Women! Don't send your sons and sweethearts to the battlefield!"

Constitutional Issues

The problem of peace and war is directly related to constitutional issues, because both rearmament and military commitment to the United States through the security treaty are directly related to features of the present constitution. Article 9 of the Constitution states:

Aspiring sincerely to an international peace based on justice and order, the Japanese people forever renounce war as a sovereign right of the nation, and the threat or use of force as means of settling international disputes.

In order to accomplish the aim of the preceding paragraph, land, sea and air forces, as well as other war potential, will never be maintained. The right of belligerency of the state will not be recognized.

(This is the official translation. A more accurate rendering of the last sentence would be "The right of the state to engage in war will not be recognized.")

This apparently unequivocal rejection of the maintenance of all "war potential" naturally raises the question of whether the existing Self-Defense Force (SDF) is constitutional or not. This problem has been debated ever since the Force was created by the occupation authorities in 1950, at the time of the Korean War. With the passage of time, the Japanese people have become accustomed to the existence of this "illegitimate" military force, and the percentage of those who approve the *fait accompli* has been increasing. At the end of 1968, only 17 percent of the respondents to an *Asahi* poll[8] thought that the existence of the SDF infringed the Constitution, while 40 percent thought that it did not.

Acceptance of the SDF does not necessarily imply approval of the maintenance of a full-fledged army, navy, and air force, since many of those who thought the SDF did not contravene the Constitution held the view that it was, or should be, something other than a *military* force. For instance, a *Yomiuri* poll at the end of 1968 produced the following results: To the question "How should we deal with the present Self-Defense Force?" the answers were: "We should strengthen it," 12.3 percent; "we should abolish it," 6.0 percent; "we should keep it as it is," 43.6 percent; and "we should transform it into a construction corps," 26.3 percent. Even among those who hold that the SDF should remain as it is, there are many who think that its raison d'être is not military action, but chiefly rescue work at times of disaster. For instance, 80 percent of the interviewees in a 1966 government survey thought that "the Self-Defense Force is most useful for "rescue work and other nonmilitary cooperation in civilian life."[9]

If the majority of Japanese are not in favor of maintaining full-fledged military forces or of strengthening the present Self-Defense Force, then the question naturally arises of how Japan's security is to be guaranteed. The *Yomiuri* poll indicates that answers to the question "What do you think is the best way to guarantee Japan's security?" were: "To place reliance on diplomacy, and not on armaments," 28.6 percent; "to maintain the security treaty between the United States and Japan," 16 percent; "to strengthen the Self-Defense Force," 6.9 percent; and "to rely on the UN or a regional collective security system," 17.7 percent. Another poll conducted in 1968 by the *Tokyo Shimbun*[10] produced similar results: "By maintaining the security treaty," 16.7 percent; "by strengthening the Self-Defense Force," 15.1 percent; "by the UN," 30.4 percent; and "by a policy of unarmed neutrality," 20.3 percent.

One vocal section of opinion claims that Japan has only been safe without normal military forces in the current international situation because of the protection afforded by the American bases maintained in Japan under the security treaty. It is obviously futile to attempt to answer the hypothetical question of whether Japan would have been able to survive without American bases, but it is useful to consider the way the Japanese feel about the American forces in Japan.

According to the 1968 *Asahi* poll, to the question "In order to defend Japan, would we do better to depend on alliance with the United States or to maintain neutrality?" 24 percent said, "depend on the

United States," while 58 percent were in favor of neutrality. Only 7 percent of the interviewees thought the American forces in Japan were there at Japan's request for her defense. Fifty-four percent thought they were there for the benefit of the United States. To the question "Do you think that the American forces stationed in Japan are necessary for her defense?" 28 percent answered Yes, and 56 percent answered No. A majority (59 percent) rejected the view that "although the existence of American bases creates nuisances, such as noise, accidents, prostitution, and the molestation of women by GIs, we should put up with them because the bases are for the defense of Japan." A somewhat smaller majority (51 percent) do not think that the United States can really be counted on to defend Japan in an emergency.

A related issue is the problem of nuclear weapons. To the question "Should Japan shelter under the American 'nuclear umbrella'?" 23.5 percent answered Yes, while 53.5 percent answered No. Indeed, 67 percent think that the American nuclear umbrella actually endangers Japan, while only 12 percent are reassured by its presence. To the question of whether Japan would be safer if she had nuclear weapons, 21.4 percent think she would, while 55.6 percent think she would not. Seventy-four percent of the interviewees in the *Tōkyō Shimbun* poll thought that Japan should maintain her security by her own efforts. Nevertheless, 49.7 percent thought that even a defensive war is not permissible. These data leave no doubt but that the "peace" constitution has taken root so deeply that there is widespread popular antipathy to war of any sort.

A similar comment may be made about other postwar reforms. For instance, to the question (in the *Yomiuri* poll) "Among the various institutional reforms of th postwar period, which do you approve of most strongly?" the most frequent answer was the enfranchisement of women (26.1 percent), second was the abolition of conscription (18.6 percent), third was labor legislation (11.1 percent), and fourth was land reform (10.5 percent). This would seem to mean that although these reforms were originally "imposed," they are now accepted by the Japanese as valuable legacies of the occupation. If we consider this sort of appraisal of the occupation reforms together with the emergence of movements to defend civil liberties and other interests, it can safely be said that the popular attitude of today is more than simple acceptance of "imposed" reforms. The *Mainichi* poll reveals that to the question "Which is the most effective method of defending your interests?" 17 percent answered "joining with those who have common interests to form a new organization," 39 percent would rely on existing organizations, and 22 per cent answered that they advocate an individual approach to government or company officials.

Such attitudes and opinions should not be regarded as isolated phenomena because they represent only the active part of the broader population which is in favor of the present Constitution. The *Asahi* poll at the end of 1968 showed that only 19 percent favored revision of the Constitution to allow Japan to have full-fledged military forces, whereas 64 percent opposed it. One tendency worth noting here is that a higher percentage opposed revision of the Constitution in the younger, more educated, and more urbanized sector of society than in other sectors. This is one of the factors that must be taken into account in trying to foresee future trends.[11]

On the other hand, those who are not in favor of revision of the Constitution are not always active in defending it. Not a few of them are interested simply in enjoying the peaceful life it guarantees. This passive attitude is partly due to the influence of the tradition that puts emphasis on harmony within society (even though passive obedience to the government helped to bring about war) and partly due to political apathy resulting from the privatization of interests in a mass society.

Although the popular desire for a peaceful life may indeed serve as a social buttress to the "Peace" Constitution, it is still too early to judge whether or not this interest will be the source of increasingly active political participation in the defense of the Constitution and the realization of its ideals.

Opinion on Foreign Affairs

There is broader popular concern with foreign affairs in Japan than in many other developed nations—in part, no doubt, because of the high degree of literacy and the wide circulation of newspapers of relatively good quality. The Japanese are so comparatively well informed that foreign affairs are an important subject of popular discussion. The war in Vietnam, as noted above, is one issue which has attracted popular attention. Answers to the question (in the *Yomiuri* poll conducted in 1968) "How would you like the war in Vietnam to end?" were as follows: "In favor of North Vietnam (and the NLF)," 5.7 percent; "in favor of the United States (and South Vietnam)," 2.8

percent; "in such a way that neither side loses face," 44.5 percent; "doesn't matter how, just as long as it ends," 30.1 percent; "don't mind if the war continues," 0.5 percent; "don't know" and no answer, 16.4 percent.

Among foreign policy issues, the China problem naturally attracts most popular attention, because of China's geographical proximity and cultural affinity. The question of trade relations has given economic importance to the China problem. In the *Yomiuri* poll, the answers to the question "What should the Sino-Japanese relationship be, taking into account the U.S.–Japanese relationship?" were: "It should remain as it is," 9.5 percent; "we should strengthen friendly relations," 36.0 percent; "we should normalize diplomatic relations," 24.7 percent; "we should not commit ourselves too far," 9.2 percent.

Obviously, the Sino-Japanese relationship is closely related to that between the United States and Japan, which has, up till now, been the most important foreign policy issue. As expansion of the Japanese economy increases national confidence, there is both a growing desire to be more independent of American foreign policy and rising impatience with the government's adherence to the American line, as in the case of policy toward China. The existence of the security treaty and the presence of American bases in Japan are China's major targets of criticism. Many Japanese realize this. For instance, the *Asahi* poll shows that, presented with the view that "The presence of American military forces in Japan hinders Japan's maintenance of friendly relations with neighboring countries," 33 percent agreed, while only 4.3 percent disagreed.

This problem of American bases naturally leads to that of the security treaty. As is well known, the treaty comes up for review in 1970 (this is being written in 1969). Thereafter, the treaty can be terminated on one year's notice by either side. As 1970 approaches, the treaty issue is becoming the most serious foreign policy problem in present-day Japan. According to the *Asahi* poll, the range of public opinion concerning it is as follows: "We should renew the treaty for another ten years," 4 percent; "we should allow it to continue, and rely on American forces," 15 percent; "we should revise the treaty so that American forces may be stationed in Japan only in an emergency," 13 percent; and, the most frequent answer, "we should direct our efforts toward its abolition," 42 percent.

From the end of the Pacific War to the outbreak of the Vietnam

War, the United States invariably topped the list of nations the Japanese liked best. But the popularity of America in Japan has been greatly undermined by the Vietnam War. In May 1963, for example, about one-half of the Japanese people named the United States as the country they liked best.[12] This percentage began to decline as the war in Vietnam went on, until finally Switzerland took the place of the United States in an opinion survey conducted in January 1967 by the semi-official Central Survey Institute. The percentages were 36.8 for Switzerland, 35.1 for the United States, 29.8 for Britain, and 27.8 for France.[13] The popular image of Switzerland in Japan has been that of a peaceful neutralist country ever since the book *Switzerland, An Earthly Paradise*[14] was published in 1904. In the *Yomiuri* poll, when the interviewees were asked "If you could be born again, which country would you choose to be born in?" Switzerland (12.7 percent) came second to Japan (57.3 percent) in the list of the countries mentioned.

Along with the security treaty issue, the problem of Okinawa has undoubtedly attracted a great deal of attention among foreign policy issues. Despite the fact that a quarter of a century has already passed since the end of the war, Okinawa is still outside the area of Japanese constitutional authority. Nor did the postwar reforms under the occupation apply to the islands. The great gulf between Japan proper and Okinawa in terms of standards of living, educational and employment opportunities, and the guarantee of civil liberties has made the people of Okinawa feel that "reversion," the termination of American administrative control and the restoration of full Japanese sovereignty, is a necessary condition for the solution of these problems. This feeling has been so strong among the people of Okinawa that the Japanese government has been forced to recognize and act on the problem.

Until recently, mainland Japanese were not much interested in the situation in Okinawa—not simply because of the physical distance, but also because of the legal position: For instance, in order to visit Okinawa, a Japanese must obtain a permit issued by the American administration. "Leftists" have had great difficulty in obtaining permits to enter the islands. Nowadays, however, a greater national confidence and an increased desire to be independent of American foreign policy, together with the fervent appeal of the people of Okinawa, have made "reversion" a national issue.

The basic policy lines of the United States concerning Okinawa were illustrated by Lieutenant General Watson, former High Commissioner of the Ryukyu Islands: "Loss of administrative rights would reduce or destroy the freedom of our military forces to act, and would seriously impair the usability of Okinawa as a base in defense of free world interests."[15] This view has always been supported by the Japanese government. The Satō-Johnson communiqué issued in Washington on January 13, 1965, "recognized the importance of United States military installations [in Okinawa] for the security of the Far East."[16]

The Japanese government has tried to find a way to reconcile American policy and Japanese popular opinion. However, the strong desire among Japanese for "reversion" was not satisfied by the government's "separation formula," under which Japan would exercise administrative control over nonmilitary areas and functions and the United States would be permitted to maintain a military base. The aim of "immediate total reversion" has been embraced by the majority of Okinawans. The first popular election of the governor (*shuseki*) in 1968 was won by the opposition candidate, who based his campaign on advocacy of this course.

Opinion in Japan proper differs not about the necessity of "reversion," which is taken for granted, but largely about how to deal with the American bases when Okinawa is returned to Japan. The range of opinion, according to the *Yomiuri* poll, is as follows: "All bases should be removed," 30.2 percent; "the bases should have the same status as those in Japan proper," 41.9 percent; "the bases should be permitted, but the presence of nuclear weapons should not be allowed," 7.3 percent; and "even the presence of nuclear weapons should be tolerated," 2.9 percent. Thus more than 72 percent of the respondents want either to abolish the military bases on Okinawa or to put them on the same footing as those in Japan proper.

As the result of the talks between President Nixon and Prime Minister Satō in November 1969, "it was agreed that the mutual security interests of the United States and Japan could be accommodated within arrangements for the return of the administrative rights over Okinawa to Japan."[17] If, however, military bases continue to occupy 23 percent of the main island,[18] the difficulty of the people will remain much the same. As long as Okinawa continues to be the "keystone" for American military strategy in the Far East, and if the issue of nuclear arms is not made explicit, then the aggravating points will be unchanged.

Thus, despite the Nixon-Satō talks, the people's discontent may remain. How far this desire for the abolition of military bases will be
realized depends on the government's stand vis-à-vis the United
States government and also on the international situation.

What has been described so far is the present state of popular opinion; how it is to be articulated in real politics is another matter.

11

Japan in the World

The United States and Japan

In the age of the satellite, Japan cannot remain isolated from the rest of the world. She has become deeply involved economically, politically, and culturally in the world situation. The increase in trade with other countries is one gauge of economic involvement in the world. In 1969, Japan's total exports amounted to $15.9 billion, and imports to $15.0 billion, an increase of 142 percent and 89 percent, respectively, over 1964.

Before the war, the Asian market provided the biggest outlet for Japanese goods. Continental China, India, and Indonesia alone took 40 percent of Japan's total exports. Asia also ranked first among Japan's suppliers, providing an average of 36.6 percent of all imports. Today, however, Japan's biggest single trade partner is the United States, which in 1969 took $4.9 billion worth of goods from Japan, or 31.0 percent of her total exports. Japan, in turn, bought $4.0 billion worth of goods from the United States, amounting to 27.2 percent of Japan's total imports. Japan is the United States' best customer after Canada. North America accounted for 34.0 percent of Japan's exports and 31.6 percent of her imports in 1969, while Asia took 33.8 percent of total exports and supplied 30.4 percent of imports. Exports to Western Europe accounted for 12.9 percent of the total, and Western Europe supplied 19.9 percent of Japan's imports.

Politically, Japan, as a member of the United Nations, has had close

diplomatic relations with other members. She has concluded bina-
tional treaties with 80 countries, and joined in 176 multinational
treaties. Particularly important among these is the security treaty with
the United States, which is Japan's only military alliance. Under this
treaty, the United States has the right to maintain military bases (about
140 in number in 1968) and to station troops (about 35,000 men in
1968) in Japan.

In terms of the exchange of people, the number of foreigners who
entered Japan in 1968 was 418,522, more than four times as many as
in 1958. Among foreigners who entered Japan in 1968, approximately
45 percent were from the United States, 27 percent from Asian countries, and 16 percent from Europe. Among Japanese who went abroad
in 1968, 52 percent went to Asian countries, 24 percent to the United
States, and 15 percent to Europe.[1]

If we consider these extensive relations between the United States
and Japan, we can see that Professor E. O. Reischauer is correct in
concluding his book *The United States and Japan* with the statement:
"Japan's future depends far more on the United States than on any
other foreign nation, and conversely America's future, at least during
the next two or three decades, may depend more on Japan than on any
other country in Asia."[2]

This close relationship between the two countries is, however,
double-edged: On the one hand, many Japanese want to maintain the
existing relations; on the other hand, not a few Japanese are made to
feel uncomfortable by Japan's dependence on the United States. Particularly serious in the view of the latter is Japan's political and military alliance with the United States, which, they believe, means that
Japan must remain a junior partner. The more sophisticated intellectuals distinguish between Japan's military commitment and economic and cultural relations, so that criticism of the one does not
imply opposition to improvement in the other. In their view, economic and cultural exchange, which is reciprocal by nature, should
not and cannot be abolished; and if Japan had no military commitment
to the United States, there would be no hindrance to the development
of a really friendly relationship.

If we reflect on the historical background of the present relationship
between the two countries, this view seems to have considerable justi-
fication. It was Commodore Perry's "black ships," as they were called
by the Japanese, which opened the doors of feudal Japan to the world

in 1853. Again in 1945, General MacArthur opened the doors of Imperial Japan by means of overwhelming military power. During the period between these two events, Japan was culturally oriented more toward Europe than toward the United States, and economically had closer relations with the countries of Asia than with the United States. The United States and Japan, neighbors who face each other across the broadest ocean in the world, often fell into power struggles over both China and the Pacific. This situation led to the catastrophic war of 1941–1945.

The second opening of Japan by the United States was followed by the postwar reforms ordered by the occupation authorities. The result of imitation of American models by Japanese political and economic leaders (previously, they had taken Germany as their pattern), and of institutional reforms based on American originals, was overwhelming American influence on every aspect of national life, including the cultural field. Nevertheless, partly because of the memory of the occupation and the continunig presence of American bases, and partly because of the American position as a superpower in the contemporary world, the Japanese image of the United States as a great power in terms of military strength still survives. This is one of the most important causes of the ambivalence in Japanese attitudes toward the United States: on the one hand, dependence; on the other, disapproval. These attitudes toward the United States are related to Japanese attitudes toward other Asian or non-Western countries: self-confidence and pride as a strong ally of the United States and a partner to her in terms of military power. But Japan's awareness of being an inferior partner in the alliance, which has its roots in memories of the bombing and the occupation, contributes to the sympathy of the Japanese for nationalist movements in developing countries, such as the NLF in South Vietnam.

It is difficult to sum up the American image of Japan. If we compare the comments on a century's modernization of Japan that appeared in American newspapers with those that appeared in European papers, we see that the American comments are less critical, putting emphasis on industriousness and other factors contributing to rapid modernization;[3] whereas the European papers commented on the dangers of group loyalty and the lack of individualism.[4] This emphasis on Japanese industriousness may give a clue to the American popular image of Japan. On the other hand, in American comments, there is some uneasiness about the uncertainty of Japan's political role in future world politics.[5] This feeling may spring from an appreciation of American national interests, which demand that Japan should play a larger part in Asian affairs and so allow America to modify her present role.

China and Japan

Although Japan has no diplomatic relations with the People's Republic of China, trade relations between the two countries have gradually increased (despite the 10 percent decrease between 1966 and 1967, probably a result of the Cultural Revolution in China). In 1961 Japan exported $16.6 million worth of goods to China and imported $40.9 million worth, while in 1966 the figures had risen to $315 million and $406.2 million, respectively.[6] In 1968, although exports increased to $326 million, imports decreased to $224 million, probably because of political circumstances. Trade with China still amounts to a smaller percentage of total trade than it did before the war (approximately 3 percent of total exports and imports in 1966, versus 24 percent of exports and 14 percent of imports in 1936, including Manchuria).[7]

The interchange of persons has been much more limited because of the lack of diplomatic relations. In 1967, 1,526 Japanese went to China, while only 150 Chinese were allowed to enter Japan. The number of Chinese visitors to Japan has fallen sharply from the level of 1964–1966 (between 500 and 600) almost to the level of 1962 (78), but the number of Japanese visitors to China has shown a more or less steady increase (in 1960 the number was 629). The Japanese desire more strongly than any other people to increase trade with China. A world poll on increased Chinese trade, published in the New York Herald Tribune on May 18, 1958, produced the following figures:[8]

	Favorable	Opposed	No Opinon
Japan	82%	3%	15%
Britain	60	16	24
Australia	59	25	16
Italy	49	13	38
Netherlands	48	18	34
France	47	10	43

In spite of this strong approval of trade relations, Japan has been preceded by Britain and France in recognition of China, and will almost certainly be preceded by Canada and Italy. The Japanese government has maintained the principle of "separation between political and economic affairs," which the Chinese government regards as unacceptable and which is thus a hindrance to the improvement of trade relations between the two countries. The Japanese people's impatience with the gulf between their wish to increase trade and normalize diplomatic relations with China and the present "unnatural" relationship has been indicated by many public opinion polls, some of which have already been mentioned.[9]

This popular attitude has its roots in the historical contact Japan has had with China for more than sixteen centuries. Almost from the beginning of Japanese history down to the end of the Tokugawa shogunate, China exerted a predominant influence on Japanese culture. China was for many centuries a great power with a highly advanced civilization. Even today, Japan's daily life is enriched by what she has learned from China. The adoption of Chinese characters to write the Japanese language is a notable example. The use of Chinese characters makes the Japanese people feel culturally akin to the Chinese; and the Chinese classics have had an influence on the mind of the Japanese similar to that of the Greek and Latin classics on the Western mind.

After the Meiji Restoration, because of Japan's "success" in rapid modernization, an attitude of arrogant superiority toward China replaced the feeling of inferiority that had been the result of cultural indebtedness. Japan's victory in the Sino-Japanese War (1894–1895) gave rise to frequent expressions of contempt for China, which had "failed" in unification and modernization. Since 1945, many Japanese have felt that Japan treated China (which had never invaded Japan, although it had been a much more powerful nation, and lay just across the East China Sea) unjustly. Also, not a few Japanese feel that China treated them with unexpected generosity at the time of the surrender, exemplified by the strict discipline of the Chinese Communist troops, who were remarkable for their good behavior, unlike the Soviet troops in Manchuria.

This feeling is not particularly strong among younger Japanese, who have no experience of World War II, but it is still important if we contrast it with that of many Americans, who tend to feel that with the Communist victory, they "lost" China. They had always been well disposed toward the Chinese people, and had tried to help them in the fields of education and social welfare, particularly through the work of missionaries. The Japanese, especially younger people, who have relatively few memories of the war, tend to think of relations with China in more realistic terms: they are concerned with questions of trade and of peace.

China's nuclear weapons are an additional factor which any Japanese, as a neighbor of China, has to take into account. But the Japanese feel that the threat of Chinese nuclear weapons is indirect, a function of increased tension between China and the United States. An opinion poll taken in November 1964 by a semigovernmental agency indicated that 29.4 percent of the respondents believed that a recent Chinese nuclear test had increased the danger to Japan's security, while 31.6 percent did not think so ("Don't know," 39.0 percent).[10] For the majority of Japanese, the Chinese nuclear threat is neither immediate nor even real. Rather, it is overshadowed by, and entangled with, the deeper concern over the escalation of the war in Vietnam, which might lead to a Sino-American war and endanger the peaceful life of the Japanese. For instance, an *Asahi* poll of 1965 reveals that to the question "Some say that if the war in Vietnam escalates, there is a danger of large-scale war between great powers like the United States and China, and others say that there is no such danger—which view do you agree with?" 57 percent of the respondents answered that there was such a danger, while 20 percent said that there was not (other answers, 3 percent; no answer, 20 percent).

Fear of war between China and the United States is, of course, strengthened by China's nuclear armaments. But the majority of Japanese, including many conservative politicians, do not really believe that China would invade Japan directly. Nor is there much likelihood, in the present state of economic prosperity, of the Japanese political situation lapsing into hopeless confusion, so there is little probability of Mao Tse-tung's ideas being widely adopted without modification. What is written and said by Chinese leaders, however, may be interpreted as being "belligerent." The Chinese feel strong indignation against the Japanese, who through the security treaty tolerate the military might of America represented by the bases. Many Japanese know from their contact with the Chinese that the leaders are, despite their published rhetoric, realistic and flexible in solving problems. For instance, trade relations between China and Japan have continued, although at a low level, even in the absence of diplomatic relations. At first, the hindrance to trade was the Chinese principle of "non-separation" between political and economic affairs. This principle has never been officially abandoned by the Chinese, but even so, trade relations were established and have been maintained. Chinese leaders have often criticized Prime Minister Satō for being too pro-American and imperialist. On the other hand, they have continued trade negotiations with conservative (government party) Diet members.

The Japanese government has taken pragmatic advantage of Peking's realistic attitude, but because Japanese leaders lack any conception of a positive role for Japan in Asia, trade negotiations have to be renewed ad hoc year after year, and no stable relationship with China has been achieved. If Japanese leaders had wanted to act more positively than they actually did to ease tensions between China and the United States, they would have been able to do something to improve the situation by making use of their contact with China. They might have provided the Americans and the Chinese with an opportunity to meet, formally or informally, in Japan, or made an effort to bring China into the United Nations.[11]

One difficulty in the way of establishing diplomatic relations with the People's Republic of China (PRC) is the already existing relationship with Taiwan, since the Taiwan government refuses to maintain diplomatic relations with any country that recognizes the PRC. But economic connections with the PRC are already more important to Japan than those with Taiwan. Even the very limited trade with the PRC that exists in the absence of diplomatic relations sometimes (3.22 percent of all imports and exports in 1966 and 2.4 percent of exports and 1.6 percent of imports in 1969) exceeds trade with Taiwan (2.61 percent of exports and 1.55 percent of imports in 1966 and 3.8 percent of exports and 1.2 percent of imports in 1969).

As for the future, the PRC, with a population fifty times as great as that of Taiwan, is a much more promising trade partner. Of course, trade relations are not the only factor to be considered in deciding foreign policy. But at least it can safely be said that Japan is in the greater bargaining position, since any damage to either diplomatic or trade relations would hurt Taiwan more than Japan.

The existence of a "Taiwan lobby," which has vested interests in trade with Taiwan, is politically important, since not a few prominent politicians, particularly members of the old guard, are connected with

it. Those who favor maintaining diplomatic relations with Taiwan
insist that Japan is bound by a promise made in 1951 in a letter from
the then Prime Minister, Shigeru Yoshida, to John Foster Dulles that
Japan would not recognize the Communist government in Peking.
The validity of this promise has been disputed both inside and outside
the Diet, and it would certainly seem to be unusual for a single personal letter to be considered binding on Japan for more than eighteen
years.

Asia, Europe, and Japan

Japan's relations with other Asian countries are closer than those with
Europe in terms of trade and interchange of persons. Japan's image of
Asia, however, is not as clear as her image of Europe, which she has
taken as a model for over a century. Although the influence of America has become strong since the end of the war, Europe still provides
the Japanese with models, particularly in the cultural field. When a
1964 poll asked where interviewees would choose to live if they could
live anywhere they liked, 52 percent said they would live in Japan,
while 31 percent wanted to live in foreign countries, among which
America and Europe were equally popular (12 percent each). Interestingly enough, the more highly educated the respondents, the higher
the percentage preferring Europe to America.[12] This would seem to
support the view that it is European "culture" that commands respect
in Japan, while America is taken as the model for a life of material
comfort.

The Japanese image of Europe has been consistent (except during
the war), but the Japanese image of Asia has undergone change. Since
the beginnings of modern Japan, there has existed a popular sense of
Asian solidarity often called "Great Asianism." Originally, this meant
solidarity among Asian countries in the face of dominance and coloni-
zation by Western powers. But the anti-Western feeling present in
Great Asianism was often entangled with nationalist sentiment, which
was in favor of expansionist policies even toward neighbors in Asia.
This tendency reached its extreme manifestation during the last war,
which was called the "Great Asian War" in the concept of the
"Greater East Asian Co-Prosperity Sphere." The idea was ambiguous,
and this slogan was understood in different ways.

For Rightists or ultranationalists, the idea served to justify the war by explaining it as a struggle by Asians, under the leadership of the Japanese, against Western invasion. Some ex-Marxists interpreted the concept as evidence that it was a war against imperialism in the Marxian sense. In this way they could justify both the war and their conversion to nationalism. Nazi ideologues understood the slogan as an application of the German *Geopolitik*, a demand for *Lebensraum*. Whatever the interpretation, what was actually achieved under this slogan was the establishment of Japanese hegemony in Asia, including occupation by Japan of several Asian countries. However, the war sometimes encouraged movements for independence from the colonial powers, as in the case of Indonesia.

After the defeat, the Japanese view of Westerners as "brutal aggressors" underwent a sudden change, and the old view of them as teachers of democracy and advanced culture returned to favor. At the same time, Japan's positive image of Asia greatly weakened: Very often "Asia" to the Japanese simply means an underdeveloped area. No clear image of Asia, or of Japan's role in Asia, has yet been reestablished. It is hardly surprising, then, that a clear image of Japan should be lacking among Asian peoples. There has been very little to replace their wartime image of Japan, and it is one reason why bitter memories of the war still remain, for example, in the Philippines.

In spite of this negative view, relations between Japan and other Asian countries have become closer. Apart from trade and the interchange of persons, the weight given to Asia in Japan's foreign aid policy is evidence of this tendency. About two-thirds of the total has been devoted to Asia in the past; and in 1969, when foreign aid amounted to $1,263 million, this trend was further emphasized, with about 74 percent of governmental aid and about 77 percent of private aid going to Asian countries. Improved economic cooperation, however, is not sufficient to establish a new image of Japan in Asia, where memories of Japanese economic policies also date from World War II.

Suspicion of Japan's "economic aggression" has been particularly strong in South Korea, which was a Japanese colony until the end of the war. When the Korean and Japanese governments established diplomatic relations in 1965, they both faced serious opposition movements. The chief reasons for the opposition were that the treaty between the two countries made unification of the two Koreas more difficult, and that the economic cooperation which followed the treaty would profit some politicians and businessmen in the two countries, but would result in the exploitation of cheap labor in Korea. Student demonstrations took place in both countries, and a boycott of Japanese products was organized in Korea. Moreover, the fact that the chairman of the Japanese delegation gave vent to some contemptuous remarks made the negotiations more difficult.

So long as this sort of arrogant attitude survives (even though chiefly among old Rightists), Japan will not be trusted by her neighbors. Although prime ministers have often said that Japan should play the role of a bridge between East and West, much more must be done to decide the real purpose of the bridge. After her success in "escaping from the East," Japan has had difficulty in finding her place in Asia.

Japan lacks a well-defined concept of her own role in Asia, and yet because of the almost complete lack of raw materials in Japan, she is relying upon her Asian neighbors through economic expansion. Tension and military force will hinder and prevent the acquisition of raw materials, as was evident in Japan's prewar predicament, while peace will enhance and maintain the constant vital flow of necessary raw materials.

Increased Japanese armament may increase her prestige, but will surely arouse serious fear and suspicion among her Asian neighbors. Even within Japan, the argument has been advanced that in order to counterbalance Chinese nuclear bombs, Japan should work toward nuclear armaments—but because she is very small, after one nuclear attack she will be unable to avenge herself. A more positive and active program of diplomatic relations can better assure Japan's security than military alliances, because of her geographical relationship to the three major superpowers.

How much Japan can do at the present is not so important as the question of in which direction Japan will move, however slow the change may be. In fact, because of the great gulf between government policy and public opinion, which has existed for a long time, radical change cannot be expected. One alternative for Japan is to strengthen her own military forces and increase her military commitment to the United States to replace the American burden in Asia. If Japan goes further in this direction, the move will provoke a Chinese response and hence increase tension in Asia. Another choice is to decrease or at least not to increase Japanese armaments and military commitments to the American Asian strategy so as to ease the tension. Since international relations are reciprocal, even a small step toward the easing of tension will result in the improvement of the situation even though the change may be gradual.

By showing that she respects the spirit of Article 9 of her Constitution, which renounces war, Japan may come to be trusted as a peaceful neighbor by the countries of Asia. If Japan can go further and play a more positive role in easing international tension in Asia by working toward unarmed neutrality, it is certain she will be able to contribute a great deal not only to the peace of Asia, but also to the peace of the world. Since unarmed neutrality has never before been tried, it is bound to be a difficult experiment; such a policy also cannot be carried out immediately. Nevertheless, it is worthwhile for Japan to make the effort.

Besides her "Peace" Constitution, there are other advantages peculiar to Japan. First, being surrounded by the sea, Japan is in no danger of being involved in boundary disputes. Second, the Japanese people have been deeply influenced by the peace-loving tradition of Buddhism. (Although, of course, the recent period of militarism cannot be dismissed as a mere aberration, since the fanatical wartime attitudes were a product of the Japanese tradition of emphasizing harmony within the nation, and of fusing the concept of harmony with that of peace.)[13] What is lacking is creative political leadership to articulate public opinion, which is committed to peace, in such a way that the spirit of the Constitution is realized in practical policies.

Japan in Comparison

Various characteristics of Japanese society have been described, and readers may interpret them in different ways. Some may be impressed with the uniqueness of Japanese society, while others may find many phenomena common to all highly industrialized societies. And it may well be best to leave interpretation to the reader.

By way of a conclusion, however, I should like to add a summary of the characteristics of Japanese society compared with other societies. There are two questions that are often asked: one is whether Japan has been or can be fully Westernized, and the other is whether Japan can serve as a model for developing non-Western countries. The two questions are based upon an assumption of unilinear development inappropriate for a comparative study. Japan can never be a Western country, nor can developing countries be Japan, because of differences of culture and other historical conditions. Each country must develop in its own way. This does not mean, however, that there is no way of comparing different societies. It suggests rather that the comparison should be multidimensional and should not ignore the uniqueness of each society.

Also important is the analysis of the mode of combination among various characteristics. For instance, from one point of view the Japanese way of life has been highly Westernized, and has many characteristics common to developed Western countries, such as urbanization, mass communications, and consumption orientation. But this does not necessarily mean that there has been a decline in traditional elements, which can survive even rapid Westernization. On the contrary, the existence of traditional elements such as group conformity has often increased the speed of Westernization. In Japan, some Western phenomena appear in an exaggerated form: For example, urban problems are greater, and the "interconsumer demonstration effect" more marked, than in most Western countries. Technological development in particular, which originated in Western developed societies, is surprisingly rapid in Japan, so that very often the means of controlling it and its effect on human life lag behind the development itself. Thus some important problems emerge in Japan even earlier, and in an even more extreme form, than in Western societies. In this sense Western readers would find it instructive to consider Japan as a case of an excessively "developed" society.

Whether one likes it or not, rapid development in Japan cannot be reversed. Even reducing the speed of development is a difficult task, because many Japanese feel that rapid development is a "normal" situation. On the other hand, partly *because* of the rapidity of development, a traditional residue has remained, and has sometimes even been used to spur development. The problems due to the traditional residue have also been intensified. Lack of individualism, which is the corollary of dependence on the group, is an example. Developing countries would have to take these difficulties into account if they were to try to follow the Japanese road.

Extremely rapid development in Japan, which resulted in her complete recovery from the devastation of the war and in greater economic prosperity than ever before, has aggravated the difficulties by combining those due to excessive development, such as intense competition, and those due to the traditional residue, such as group conformity. For example, fierce competition in the automobile industry produces far too many cars for Japan's antiquated road system and contributes to the high accident rate. The recent student revolts are the result in part of the fact that Japanese universities on the one hand lack modern management, and on the other suffer all the difficulties of the "multiversity." In Japanese universities there is a curious combination of highly developed science, which is capable, for example, of producing space rockets, and traditional, even premodern, methods of management.

Student revolts (in Japan and elsewhere) are not simply the product of the difficulties within the universities. They very often reflect widespread discontent throughout the nation. This is one reason why not a few Japanese are sympathetic to them, although students are much more isolated from other sectors of society than in the United States. Foreign policy issues, such as the security treaty between the United States and Japan and the problem of Okinawa, are important elements in the students' "cause."

This widespread discontent is not always directed at specific objects. A vague feeling of being alienated in a "stagnant" society is often a source of discontent. Curiously enough, despite rapid change, many people feel that the present situation is stagnant, because they believe that the underdogs remain underdogs even though their standard of living improves. Furthermore, even people in the middle class are losing patience, because they feel they are being forced to adjust to a situation which they have no hope of changing.

The recent surprising popularity in Japan of Peter Drucker's *The Age of Discontinuity* may be interpreted in two different ways: It may be that the book is popular because it can explain and justify the rapid and radical change taking place in present-day Japan; or it may be popular because it reflects a *desire* for drastic change. More important than the question of which of these interpretations is correct (they may both be) is the fact that each reveals different aspects of the same characteristic: On the one hand there is no doubt that Japanese society is changing very rapidly; and on the other hand, the pattern of change is similar throughout society, so that many people feel that since everybody is traveling in the same direction, there is relatively no real change.

The capacity for rapid change differs from person to person and from generation to generation, and so there appear discrepancies resulting from the differences in rate of change among different sectors of society. Particularly serious is the discrepancy between generations. Differences in attitudes between different generations is common to all changing societies, but the rapidity of change and strength of group conformity in each generation have widened this gap in Japan.

One reason why the student revolt in Japan is extremely radical can be found in this generation gap. Another reason is that discontent with the present "stagnant" situation has been aggravated in the university students' generation by the knowledge that they must soon enter into lifetime employment, which to them seems to be lifetime enslavement.

Lifetime employment is peculiar to Japan, but it only intensifies a stagnation commonly found in highly developed societies. Ennui is one of the products of this stagnation. Another more active attitude toward stagnation, similar to that of Japanese students, has been expressed by an angry American student: "I intend to fight that society which lied to and smothered me for so long, and continues to do so to vast numbers of people."[14] If the unformulated discontent common among the Japanese in fact arises from resentment against such stagnation, then improvement of the standard of living alone will not solve the problem. The standard of living of Japan, measured in terms of per capita income, can be raised to the level of the most developed Western countries. But this will not be sufficient to satisfy the Japanese. The lack of a cause has given many Japanese a feeling of uncertainty.

What will give them the feeling that there is something worth living for? "My-home-ism" does not suffice. The national goal, which was once very clear and at the same time very dangerous, seems to have gone forever. Nor will this situation be confined to Japan: it is very likely to arise in other developed countries, in which there is much less consciousness of a national goal than in developing countries. The situation may have arisen earlier in Japan because of the lack of a strong religious tradition.

We have considered the way in which Japanese conditions aggravate certain problems. This aggravation could, and should, be turned to advantage. The more serious the problem, the more obvious the need for a solution. For instance, because the Japanese people experienced atomic bombing, they are extremely sensitive about any sort of nuclear weapon. Protest against the visits of nuclear submarines may seem to be evidence of excessive nervousness; but if we consider the density of population around the visited ports and the actual increases in radioactivity that have occurred during some of the visits, together with the experiences of atom bomb victims, the Japanese sensitivity is hardly surprising. A similar observation can be made about their attitude toward the war in Vietnam.

There are other problems demanding immediate solution—for example, urban congestion and its accompaniments. All such problems are partly the product of rapid technological development, and are made worse in Japan by the gap between a developed technology and the ability of society to control it. If the Japanese can find a way to bridge this gap, it would, without doubt, be a great advance for the whole human race. In order to take the first step in this direction, it is necessary for Japan to have a national goal that is not nationalistic, but based on universalistic values, such as international peace in the strict sense (that is, disarmament) and justice achieved by nonviolent means. This goal is far from the present reality, but at the same time there is the potential and a great need for such a goal among the Japanese.

In order to investigate the problem of how this popular demand can be articulated in concrete policies, we must find an appropriate way of organizing the demand. Here, we have to face the important problem of the pattern of organization. Group conformity, or "groupism," is an important characteristic of Japanese society, and an increased threat of "groupism" is a common trend in the world, as David Riesman and others have pointed out.[15] Traditional Japanese group conformity is not exactly the same as that found in other parts of the world, but nevertheless the characteristics of "groupism" described by Riesman can also be applied to the Japanese case. Indeed, this characterization probably fits Japanese society more closely than any other. Of course, the traditional lack of individualism, or inner-directedness, differentiates Japan from the West. As a result, "groupism" appears in Japan in an extreme form.

An analysis of Japanese society thus leads us to the investigation of problems common to contemporary Western societies. Individualism must be reconsidered in Japan too, even more seriously, indeed, than in Western society. Citizenship must revive or emerge in order to revitalize the democratic procedure. There are differences of degree and the way in which problems appear, but we are facing basically the same problem in all contemporary societies.

Notes

1. Introduction

1. For example, see "Year of the Open Door—*The Economist* Reconsiders Japan," *The Economist* (November 28, 1964).
2. Ruth Benedict, *The Chrysanthemum and the Sword* (London: Secker and Warburg, 1947).
3. R. P. Dore, *City Life in Japan: A Study of a Tokyo Ward* (London: Routledge and Kegan Paul, 1958), p. 49.
4. *Asahi Jānaru* (January 1, 1969).
5. Benedict, *op. cit.*, pp. 1–2.

2. Cultural Heritage and Westernization

1. Max Weber, *Gesammelte Aufsaetze zur Religionssoziologie*, Vol. II (Tuebingen: Mohr, 1923), pp. 303–4.
2. Reinhard Bendix, *Nation-building and Citizenship* (New York and London: Wiley, 1964), p. 179.
3. R. P. Dore, "The Legacy of Tokugawa Education," in Marius B. Jansen (ed.), *Changing Japanese Attitudes Towards Modernization* (Princeton, N.J.: Princeton University Press, 1965), p. 100.
4. For details, see Takeshi Ishida, "Urbanization and Its Impact on Japanese Politics," *Annals of the Institute of Social Science*, No. 8 (Tokyo: University of Tokyo, 1967), pp. 1–11.

3. "Enrich the Country and Strengthen the Military"

1. For details, see Takeshi Ishida, "Movements to Protect Constitutional Government," in George O. Totten (ed.), *Democracy in Prewar Japan* (Boston: Heath, 1965), pp. 85f.
2. Robert E. Ward, "Japan: The Continuity of Modernization," in Lucian W. Pye and Sydney Verba (eds.), *Political Culture and Political Development* (Princeton, N.J.: Princeton University Press, 1965), p. 42.
3. Suzuki Kantarō Denki Hensan Iinkai (Committee for Editing the Biography of Kantarō Suzuki), *Suzuki Kantarō Den* (*Biography of Kantarō Suzuki*) (Tokyo: Suzuki Kantarō Denki Hensan Iinkai, 1950), p. 240.

4. American Occupation

1. For details, see Hans H. Baerwald, *The Purge of Japanese Leaders Under the Occupation* (Berkeley and Los Angeles: University of California Press, 1959).
2. John D. Montgomery, *Forced to Be Free, the Artificial Revolution in Germany and Japan* (Chicago: The University of Chicago Press, 1957).
3. R. P. Dore, *Land Reform in Japan* (London and New York: Oxford University Press, 1959), p. 385.
4. For details, see Takeshi Ishida, "Development of Interest Groups and the Pattern of Political Modernization in Japan," in Robert E. Ward (ed.), *Political Development in Modern Japan* (Princeton, N.J.: Princeton University Press, 1968), pp. 331f.
5. Max Weber, *Wirtschaft und Gesellschaft, Grundriss der Verstehenden Soziologie*, Studienausgabe herausgegeben von Johannes Winckelmann, Zweiter Halbband (Köln and Berlin: Kiepernheuer & Witsch, 1964), pp. 854f.
6. For details, see Yoshinori Ide and Takeshi Ishida, "The Education and Recruitment of Governing Elites in Modern Japan," in Rupert Wilkinson (ed.), *Governing Elites, Studies in Training and Selection* (New York: Oxford University Press, 1969), pp. 108–34.

5. Values,   Norms, and Education

1. For those who are particularly interested in the historical development of a value system in premodern and modern Japan, the following two books are useful: Robert N. Bellah, *Tokugawa Religion* (New York: Free Press, 1957); Masao Maruyama, *Thought and Behavior in Modern Japanese Politics* (London: Oxford University Press, 1963).
2. R. K. Beardsley, J. W. Hall, and R. E. Ward, *Village Japan* (Chicago: The University of Chicago Press, 1959).
3. "The *Asahi* Poll on Vietnam," *Japan Quarterly*, XII, 4 (October–December 1965).
4. Physical disease is not the only problem of the victims of the atomic bombs.

More serious is the traumatic psychological impact. See, for details, Robert
J. Lifton, *Life in Death* (New York: Random House, 1968). In fact, for instance, not a few A-bomb victims do not want to be registered because of
the fear that the registration may result in difficulties at the time of marriage.
Although registration would give a person some medical privileges, if he is
known as a victim, the future partner may fear that the experience of having
been exposed to radioactivity would produce deformed children.

5. Ezra F. Vogel, *Japan's New Middle Class* (Berkeley and Los Angeles: University of California Press, 1963), p. 28.

6. According to Sōrifu Tōkeikyoku (Bureau of Statistics, Office of the Prime
Minister), *Shōwa 43nen Shūgyōkōzō Kihonchōsa Hōkokusho* (*1968 Employment
Status Survey*), p. 108, the stratification of employees by income groups is
as follows (average income is 552,000 Yen, or $1,533):

Yen (10,000)	Dollar (approx.)	Number (000)	Percentage
Less than 12	Less than 333	1,223	4.0
12–17	333–499	1,055	3.5
18–23	500–665	2,522	8.3
24–29	666–832	2,355	7.7
30–39	833–1,110	5,566	18.2
40–59	1,111–1,665	6,922	22.7
60–99	1,666–2,776	7,423	24.3
100–149	2,777–4,166	2,454	8.0
150–199	4,167–5,554	545	1.8
200 and above	5,555 and above	426	1.4
Not reported		38	0.1
Total		30,528	100.0

6. Family and Community

1. Ezra F. Vogel, *Japan's New Middle Class* (Berkeley and Los Angeles, 1963),
p. 180. This book gives useful details of family life among Japanese of the
new middle class.

2. R. P. Dore, *City Life in Japan* (London: Routledge and Kegan Paul, 1958),
p. 154. This book is also informative about family life in the city. The situation it describes has been changing rapidly since the book was written, but
it has been changing in the direction indicated by Dore.

3. *Ibid.*

4. One example of those publc opinion polls is given in Takeshi Ishida, "Popular Attitudes Toward the Japanese Emperor," *Asian Survey*, II, 2 (April
1962), 35.

5. Dore, *op. cit.*, p. 115.

6. Vogel, *op. cit.*, p. 230.

7. R. P. Dore, *Land Reform in Japan* (London and New York: Oxford Univer-

sity Press, 1959), p. 385. This book contains an excellent description and analysis not only of the process of the land reform, but also of the situation in rural communities from that time until the 1950s.

8. An account of this incident can be found in Leonard Broom and Philip Selznick (eds.), *Sociology* (New York: Row Peterson, 1957), p. 79.

9. Dore, *City Life in Japan*, pp. 253f.

10. Tokue Shibata, *Gendai Toshiron* (*Contemporary Cities*) (Tokyo: University of Tokyo Press, 1967), pp. 296, 79. Other figures in this section are also taken from this book.

7. Organizations and Institutions

1. Prince Konoe planned to establish a new national party in 1940 in an attempt to counterbalance the influence of the military clique. The militarists, however, wanted to use his popularity to secure instead an agency for ensuring total commitment to the war effort. It turned out that the IRAA, when it was established, was nothing more than a supplement to the bureaucracy, because its internal factional conflicts deprived it of independent power.

2. Edward T. Hall, *The Silent Language* (New York: Doubleday, 1959).

3. For details, see Yoshinori Ide and Takeshi Ishida, "The Education and Recruitment of Governing Elites in Modern Japan," in Rupert Wilkinson (ed.), *Governing Elites, Studies in Training and Selection* (New York: Oxford University Press, 1969).

4. Michiya Shimbori: *Gakubatsu* (Tokyo: Fukumura Shuppan, 1969), pp. 65–66. "Members of the elite" here means those who were listed in *Jinji Koshinroku* (the equivalent of *Who's Who*).

5. Shimbori, *op cit.*, pp. 66–67.

6. Hideo Shimizu, *Tokyo Daigaku Hogakubu* (*Faculty of Law, University of Tokyo*) (Tokyo: Kōdansha, 1965), p. 50.

7. In 1954, immediately after the passing of the law, 122 persons were arrested on suspicion of offering or accepting bribes. Bribes were offered in an attempt to influence the tonnage quota to be allotted by the government to each individual shipbuilding company.

8. Extreme cases are described in Takeyoshi Kawashima, *Kekkon* (*Marriage*) (Tokyo: Iwanami, 1954), p. 15.

9. See Ide and Ishida, *op. cit.*, pp. 113f.

10. The number of bills (private members' bills and government bills) introduced and passed in each session is available in Kunio Fukumoto, *Kanryō* (*Bureaucrats*) (Tokyo: Kōbundō, 1959), pp. 132–136.

11. Kanryōseido Kenkyūkai (Research Group on Bureaucracy), *Kanryō* (*Bureaucrats*) (Tokyo: San'ichi Shobō, 1959), p. 130.

12. See, for instance, Dan F. Henderson, "Law and Political Modernization in Japan," in Robert E. Ward (ed.), *Political Development in Modern Japan* (Princeton, N.J.: Princeton University Press, 1968), p. 412.

13. In 1965, 39 (8.4 percent) out of 467 members of the Lower House and 17 (6.8 percent) out of 250 members of the Upper House were lawyers. See,

Toshitaka Ushiomi (ed.), *Gendai no Hōritsuka* (*Contemporary Jurists*) (Tokyo: Iwanami, 1966), p. 147. Incidentally, the number of lawyers has been increasing. In 1969, the total number of registered lawyers was 8,562.

14. English translations of twenty-six key cases can be found in John M. Maki, *Court and Constitution in Japan: Selected Supreme Court Decisions, 1948–60* (Seattle: University of Washington Press, 1964). The conservative character of Japanese high court judges compared with their American and British counterparts can be seen, for instance, in Glendon Schubert, "Ideological Distance, a Small Space Analysis Across Three Cultures," *Comparative Political Studies*, Vol. 1, No. 3 (October 1968).

Incidentally, judges are usually more conservative than lawyers in Japan. This is proved by a survey of the attitudes of lawyers. Those who have served as judges are on the whole more conservative than those who have not. Some liberal judges have resigned in order to return to private practice, but their number is small compared with that of those who returned to legal practice after retirement. See Ushiomi, *op. cit.*, pp. 147f.

15. For details, see Takeshi Ishida, "The Development of Interest Groups and the Pattern of Modernization in Japan," in Robert E. Ward (ed.), *Political Development in Modern Japan* (Princeton, N.J.: Princeton University Press, 1968), pp. 317–30.

8. The Mass Age

1. The results are available in NHK Hōsō-chōsajo (NHK Broadcasting Research Institute), *Kokumin Seikatsujikan Chōsa* (*Research on the Use of Time in Daily Life*) (Tokyo: NHK, 1965), which is the source for most of the figures quoted in this paragraph.

2. To be more precise, there are fewer people who read books and more people who read weekly magazines among those who watch television a lot than among those who do not watch television much. For details, see Mimpōgosha Chōsakenkyūkai (Research Group of Five Commercial Channels), *Nihon no Shichōsha* (*The Japanese Audience*) (Tokyo: Seibundō-shinkōsha, 1966), pp. 90f.

3. This fact together with the number of letters to the editor was mentioned in Saburō Kageyama, *Shimbun Tōsho Ron* (*On the letters to the Editor*) (Tokyo: Nihon Jānarizumu Shuppankai, 1968), pp. 30f.

4. Mimpōgosha Chōsakenkyūkai (eds.), *op. cit.*, p. 124.

5. Mimpōgosha Chōsakenkyūkai (eds.), *op. cit.*, p. 31.

6. Mimpōgosha Chōsakenkyūkai (eds.), *op. cit.*, p. 148.

7. Kokuminseikatsu Kenkyūjo (Standards of Living Research Institute), *Daitoshi ni okeru Shōhisha no Ishiki oyobi Kodō ni kansuru Chōsa* (*Research on Behavior of Consumers in Large Cities*) (Tokyo: Kokuminseikatsu Kenkyūjo, 1961), pp. 204–7.

8. Mimpōgosha Chōsakenkyūkai (eds.), *Nihon no Shōhisha* (*The Japanese Consumer*) (Tokyo: Daiyamondosha, 1964), p. 58.

9. *Ibid.*, p. 92.
10. *Yomiuri Shimbun*, January 1, 1965.
11. Richard Hofstadter, *Anti-intellectualism in American Life* (New York: Knopf, 1962), p. 422.

9. Rapid Social Change

1. Karl Mannheim, *Diagnosis of Our Time* (London: Routledge & Kegan Paul, 1943), p. 95.
2. For more details, see Takeshi Ishida, "Urbanization and Its Impact on Japanese Politics," *Annals of the Institute of Social Science*, No. 8 (Tokyo: Institute of Social Science, University of Tokyo, 1967).
3. Kanagawa-Ken (Kanagawa Prefectural Government), *Gijutsu Kakushin to Rōshikankei* (*Technological Innovation and Labor Relations*) (Yokohama: Kanagawa Prefectural Government, 1957), pp. 3f.
4. *Yomiuri Shimbun*, January 1, 1969. The 10,000 interviewees were chosen by stratified random sampling from among people between 19 and 79 years of age.
5. Tōkyōdaigaku Sōgōkenkyūkai (Association for Interdisciplinary Research, University of Tokyo), *Gijutsu Kakushin* (*Technological Innovation*), (Tokyo: University of Tokyo Press, 1965), p. 248.
6. Sheldon S. Wolin, *Politics and Vision* (Boston and Toronto: Little, Brown, 1960), pp. 352f.
7. Ernest Barker, *Reflections on Government* (Oxford: Oxford University Press, 1942), pp. 142f.
8. For the characteristics of *"carte blanche"* leadership, see Takeshi Ishida, "The Development of Interest Groups and the Pattern of Political Modernization in Japan," in Robert E. Ward (ed.), *Political Development in Modern Japan* (Princeton, N.J.: Princeton University Press, 1968), pp. 314–15.
9. David Riesman and Nathan Glazer, "Criteria for Political Apathy," in Alvin Gouldner (ed.), *Studies in Leadership* (New York: Russell and Russell, 1965).
10. For more detail, see Takeshi Ishida, "Emerging or Eclipsing Citizenship—A Study of Change in Political Attitudes in Postwar Japan," *The Developing Economies*, VI, 4 (The Institute of Asian Economic Affairs, Tokyo, December 1968).
11. R. J. Pranger, *Eclipse of Citizenship* (New York: Harper and Row, 1968).

10. Popular Attitudes and Opinions

1. *Yomiuri Shimbun*, January 1, 1969.
2. *Asahi Jānaru*, October 13, 1968, p. 11.
3. *Asahi Shimbun*, January 8, 1967.
4. *Asahi Shimbun*, February 6, 1967.

5. *Asahi Shimbun*, February 7, 1967.
6. *Mainichi Shimbun*, January 1, 1969.
7. Kōseishō (Ministry of Health and Welfare), *Kōsei Hakusho* (*White Paper on Health and Welfare*), (Tokyo: Kōseishō, 1968), p. 57. This is, if anything, a conservative estimate.
8. Published in *Asahi Shimbun*, January 5, 1969. This poll used a random nationwide sample of 3,000 people over 20 years of age.
9. *Asahi Shimbun* Anzenhoshō Chōsakai (*Asahi Shimbun* Research Group on the Security Problem), *Nanajū-nen no Seiji Kadai* (*Political Tasks in 1970*) (Tokyo: *Asahi Shimbun*, 1967), p. 162.
10. *Tokyo Shimbun*, January 1, 1969. This poll used a random nationwide sample of 3,000 people over 20 years of age.
11. For more details, see Takeshi Ishida, "Japanese Public Opinion and Foreign Policy," *The Annals of the Institute of Social Science*, No. 9 (Tokyo: University of Tokyo, 1968).
12. *Shūkan Jiji*, June 1, 1963.
13. *Shūkan Jiji*, February 4, 1967. This was a nationwide survey of 1,250 persons over the age of 20.
14. Isoo Abe, *Chijō no Risōkoku Suisu*, published in 1904.
15. Cited in Mikio Higa, "The Reversion Theme in Current Okinawan Politics," *Asian Survey*, VII, 3 (March 1967). This article is very informative on the subject.
16. For the full text of this communiqué, see *Japan Times*, January 15, 1965.
17. Quoted from the joint communiqué of November 21, 1969.
18. Kazuhisa Ikawa and Minoru Takahashi, "Okinawa," *Tembō*, April 1970, p. 23.

II. Japan in the World

1. The figures in this paragraph are taken from Hōmushō (*Ministry of Justice*), *Shutsunyūkoku Kanri Tōkei Nempō* (*Annual Immigration Statistics*), 1968, pp. 2–3, 118–22.
2. Edwin O. Reischauer, *The United States and Japan*, rev. ed. (Cambridge, Mass.: Harvard University Press, 1961), p. 337.
3. Comments in *The New York Times*, January 2, 1969; *The Sunday Sun*, October 20, 1968; *The Philadelphia Inquirer*, October 26, 1968.
4. *The Times* (London), October 23, 1968; *Le Figaro*, October 22, 1968.
5. Comments in *The Washington Post*, October 27, 1968; *The Philadelphia Inquirer*, October 26, 1968.
6. Chūgoku Kenkyūjo (Institute of Chinese Studies), *Shin Chūgoku Nenkan* (*New China Yearbook*) (Tokyo: Tōhōshoten, 1968), p. 179.
7. *Asahi Shimbun* (eds.), *Asahi Nenkan* (*Asahi Yearbook*) (Tokyo: *Asahi Shimbun*, 1938), p. 230.
8. Douglas H. Mendel, Jr., *Japanese People and Foreign Policy* (Berkeley, Calif.: University of California Press, 1961), p. 232.

9. A nationwide opinion poll on recognition of China in July 1964 showed 35% for, 9.9% against, 55.2% don't know (*Shūkan Jiji*, August 1, 1965).

10. *Shūkan Jiji*, December 5, 1964. Incidentally, there are no figures that show the statistical magnitude of the opposition to the Chinese nuclear test, but it is a reasonable guess that if the respondents had been asked whether they approved or disapproved of the Chinese nuclear test, the majority would have answered that they disapproved. Among the grounds for this guess is an opinion poll taken by the *Yomiuri* in September 1961. *Question:* "The Soviet Union has renewed nuclear testing, and the United States also intends to do so. What do you think about nuclear tests by these two powers?" The replies: They should both stop the tests, 74%; the American test is justifiable, 1%; the Soviet Union is to blame for renewed testing, 1%; other opinions, 13%; no opinion, 11%. These results are taken from Naikaku Sōridaijin Kambō Kōhōshitsu (Information Center of the Prime Minister's Secretariat), *Zenkoku Yorochōsa no Genkyō* (*Present State of National Opinion Polls*), 1961, p. 100.

11. A nationwide opinion poll taken in December 1961 on the issue of the seating of the People's Republic of China in the United Nations gave the following results: 32.5% for, 7.6% against, 59.9% don't know. (Naikaku Sōridaijin Kambō Kōhōshitsu, *op. cit.*, p. 101).

12. *Asahi Shimbun*, December 27, 1964. This poll used a random nationwide sample of 3,000 people over 20 years of age.

13. For more details, see Takeshi Ishida, "Beyond the Traditional Concepts of Peace in Different Cultures," *Journal of Peace Research*, No. 2 (Peace Research Institute, Oslo, 1969).

14. Howard Zinn, *SNCC: The New Abolitionists* (Boston: Beacon, 1964), p. 15.

15. See, e.g., David Riesman, *Individualism Reconsidered* (New York: Macmillan, 1951).

Bibliographical Note

So many books on Japan have been published that it would be superfluous to list those which readers can easily find by referring to library catalogs. Even selecting important works is a difficult task, since selection must take particular interests into account. Here I simply list some of the works which would have significance for general readers.

For bibliographies see, Hugh Borton, Serge Elisseef, William W. Lockwood, and John C. Pelzel, *A Selected List of Books and Articles on Japan in English, French and German* (Cambridge: Harvard-Yenching Institute, 1954); and Bernard S. Silberman, *Japan and Korea: A Critical Bibliography* (Tucson: University of Arizona Press, 1962).

In order to locate more recent books, handy bibliographies are, Ministry of Foreign Affairs, Japan, *Introducing Japan through Books, A Selected Bibliography* (Tokyo: Ministry of Foreign Affairs, 1968); and Ministry of Foreign Affairs, Japan, *Readings on the Modernization of Japan, A Selected Bibliography* (Tokyo: Ministry of Foreign Affairs, 1968). These two are simply booklets for the general public and not sufficient for scholars, but one advantage is that these include books in English published in Japan.

For readings see, William T. De Bary (ed.), *Sources of the Japanese Tradition* (New York: Columbia University Press, 1958).

Some pioneer works in Japanese studies are, Ruth Benedict, *The Chrysanthemum and the Sword* (London: Secker and Warburg, 1947); Edwin O. Reischauer, *Japan: The Story of a Nation* (New York: Knopf, 1970), first published in 1947 as *Japan: Past and Present;* George Sansom, *Japan: A Short Cultural History* (London: Cresset Press, 1952); and George Sansom, *The Western World and Japan: A Study in the Interaction of European and Asiatic Cultures* (New York: Knopf, 1950).

Good general textbooks which include Japanese history are, Edwin O. Reischauer and John K. Fairbank, *East Asia: The Great Tradition* (Boston: Houghton Mifflin, 1958), and John K. Fairbank, Edwin O. Reischauer, and Albert M. Craig, *East Asia: The Modern Transformation* (Boston: Houghton Mifflin, 1965).

Among numerous academic works, particularly important examples are, Robert N. Bellah, *Tokugawa Religion; the Values of Preindustrial Japan* (New York: Macmillan, 1957), an ambitious historical and sociological approach to

Japanese Society; Ronald P. Dore, *City Life in Japan* (London: Routledge and
Kegan Paul, 1958); Ronald P. Dore, *Land Reform in Japan* (London and New
York: Oxford University Press, 1959); and Ezra F. Vogel, *Japan's New Middle
Class* (Berkeley and Los Angeles: University of California Press, 1963). These
three books were based on the authors' experiences of living in Japanese society
and buttressed by their scientific investigations. The reader will be impressed by
the detailed facts as well as their academic insights. For those who are interested
in knowing the Japanese author's analysis of his own society the following book
is recommended. Masao Maruyama, *Thought and Behaviour in Modern Japanese
Politics* (London and New York: Oxford University Press, 1963; expanded ed.,
1969).

Many others are being published, but since many of them are rather on
special subjects and since some of the most important have already been mentioned in the text, I should like to add here only some books published in Japan
which incorporate basic materials. This is partly because these books are mostly
unfamiliar to readers outside Japan, but chiefly because readers may want to
check more recent figures.

Most important are the numerous White Papers, published, in most cases
annually, by the Government Printing Office. It is sometimes said that since
these White Papers are published by the government they invariably emphasize
the bright side of Japanese society. But the figures they contain are susceptible
of different analyses, and the reader may draw from them conclusions other than
the official ones. Some examples of these White Papers are:

Keizai Hakusho	(White Paper on the Economy)
Kokuminseikatsu Hakusho	(White Paper on Standards of Living)
Kōsei Hakusho	(White Paper on Health and Welfare)
Unyu Hakusho	(White Paper on Transportation)
Kensetsu Hakusho	(White Paper on Construction)

All are published in Japanese, but English summaries of important White Papers
are included in the *Information Bulletin* published monthly by the Public Information Bureau, Ministry of Foreign Affairs.

Those information sources published by the Ministry of Foreign Affairs are
readily obtainable at Japanese embassies and consulates. Among them are *Statistical Survey of the Economy of Japan* (published annually) and *Japan Reference
Series* (occasional booklets on specific subjects, such as agriculture, the fishing
industry, and foreign investment).

*K.B.S. Bibliography of Standard Reference Books for Japanese Studies with De-
scriptive Notes* is useful for those who can read Japanese. It is published in ten
volumes by the Kokusai Bunka Shinkōkai and distributed by the University of
Tokyo Press:

1. Generalia
2. Geography and travel
3. History and biography (3 parts)
4. Religion
5. A. History of thought (2 parts), B. Education
6. A. Language; B. Literature (5 parts)
7. A. Arts and crafts; B. Theatre, dance and music
8. Manners and customs and folklore
9. A. Politics; B. Law (2 parts)
10. Economics (2 parts)

Index